RETURN TO JUDAISM

A Starting Point For Non-Religious Jews

Return To Judaism

Copyright © 2021 by Michael Apfelbaum.

All rights reserved. Printed in the United States of America. No part of this book may be used or reproduced in any manner whatsoever without written permission except in the case of brief quotations embodied in critical articles or reviews.

First Paperback Edition March 2021
Second Paperback Edition June 2021
ISBN: 978-0-578-87550-7

Publisher: Pros Inc., Boynton Beach, FL 33472

For information contact: ijwana@aol.com

TABLE OF CONTENTS

Preface vii
Chapter I: The Idiot Jew 1
Chapter II: Why Pursue Judaism? 13
Chapter III: More Reasons To Get Started 27
Chapter IV: Abraham, Moses, &
   the Ten Commandments 41
Chapter V: The Three Denominations of Judaism 53
Chapter VI: The Torah of Truth 63
Chapter VII: Torah Study Benefits 73
Chapter VIII: What Will Happen To You
   As It Happened To Me 85
Chapter IX: HASHEM: The World's
   Greatest Comedian 97
Chapter X: Idiot Rabbis 101
Chapter XI: Time 105
Chapter XII: Fun Facts About Miracles 111
Chapter XIII: Trapped Inside Secular Culture 123
Chapter XIV: Comparing Secular and
   Biblical Perspectives 133
Chapter XV: The History of Planet Earth 145
Chapter XVI: Judaism: Is It Really Such a Very,
   Very Deep Dive? 153
Chapter XVII: The Ten Suggestions: Your New Jewish
   Strengthening Program 161
Postscript 169
Addendum: The Ten Commandments 170

Preface

There is a Spark in every Jew. This Spark is the connection to HASHEM, God, which every Jew feels, whether they are observant or not. But so many non-religious Jews walking the planet today, feeling this Spark, don't know what to do to pursue it further. This book is for you. It tells you the way to get started. It tells you how and why it is in your best interest to further your Jewishness.

There is nothing new about Judaism stated within the contents of this book. All practicing Jews probably know 99% of it because it's all pretty basic. But you don't because you have been secular, non-religious your entire life. Inside you'll learn many things about Judaism that you never knew before because nobody exposed you to them. I'm sharing them with you because by knowing these "little incidentals" you will gain a better understanding of who the Jewish people are. Jews have achieved amazing things right from their beginnings and continue to achieve amazing things even today. No other group of people has made the immense moral and value contributions to the world as much as the Jews. When you are done reading "Return To Judaism" you'll understand this better. And because of this "stature" you will yearn to be more a part of it.

Imagine yourself a mother or father and you are on your deathbed surrounded by all your children and grandchildren. You try to gather in your mind everything you have lived and known in order to pass on just a couple of things you want your children to live up to. It may be as simple as "be nice." It may be, "give charity." It may be any one of hundreds of good thoughts you'd like your children to know and live by. When you pass on it's your fervent wish that those people you've brought into the world will live good lives and add to the goodness of everyone they encounter in the world.

You get to do it only once. Your husband gets to do it once. After a couple of generations your parting words and your husbands parting words will probably be lost along with even your name. Your children and their children will do the same. And their parting words and names also will be lost forever. This is the way of the world, normal and natural.

Now imagine a group of people, "allegedly" with the help of an otherworldly source, come up with "something" that they want to leave to future generations. Something that they hoped future people will live up to in order to increase goodness in their world and the world about them. But now it's not lost after a couple of generations. 2500 years ago the "Hebrews" left the Torah containing the 10 Commandments.

In fact, for over 2500 years the smartest and brightest minds study and argue about every word, combination of words, sentences, paragraphs, chapters, and books. Volumes and volumes of discussions have been passed on. All of this is to make people now and in the future happier in their lives, bringing holiness into their lives while eliminating the crude, rude aspects of everyday living. That's what Judaism is.

If your mother's last words were "be nice," wouldn't you do your best to be nice? Would that be so hard to do and wouldn't that make yourself and the world around you better? If your father's last words were, "give charity," wouldn't you do your best to give charity? Would that be so hard to do and wouldn't that make yourself and the world around you better?

So now generation after generation of Jews have left their parting words for you, and their names are not forgotten. These words will make yourself and the world around you better. It sounds pretty good to me. You've been asleep to this gift from your forefathers. It's time to wake up. It's time to become part of the goodness and pass it along, by example, to your loved ones. Some will mock you. Others will be inspired by your calm and intelligence. You accept the gift and pass it along to those who also feel the spark. The ones that don't… well, so be it.

The history of Jewish ethical thought and investigation makes me proud to be a Jew. It's made me want to be more of a part of it. It's a good thing to be a Jew. It always has been and always will be a good thing to be a Jew. I was never taught about Jewish accomplishments throughout history, especially from the spiritual point of view, so I'm looking to awaken you to them and educate you on what I missed out on for six decades. I believe your whole perspective will change and you will want to be a part of it right now. The Jew crew has been quite a cool posse for 3500 years. It's time you jumped in.

For 63 years I was a secular Jew, a self-described "Idiot Jew." My parents raised me so that I fully assimilated into American culture, became successful and well liked, but I felt empty like something was missing and things should be more meaningful. Is life all about eating steak, drinking vodka, having sex, and laying on a beach? My material success didn't come close to matching my weak emotional state. I never went to services and rarely even lit Chanukah candles. I dated non-Jewish women almost exclusively. Incredibly, my closest friends were mostly all Jewish, secular, non-religious Jews. So, I know who you are and I know you could stand to read this little Jewish primer.

My return to Judaism happened by accident and I'm still the same person I always was only more relaxed and insightful. By adding a small level of Jewish observance my lifestyle became more focused on "goodness" which is the essence of Judaism. It not only improved me but also improved the people I interacted with. I still play tennis and golf, go out with friends, and continue my old American lifestyle but with greater clarity as to what it means to do good things.

You will too. Doing a "mitzvah," a good thing, is more enthralling than a movie, more satisfying than an ice cream cone, and lasts longer than doing twenty abdominal crunches. And doing mitzvahs never gets old or boring. It becomes a way of life that gains momentum every day.

There is a "spectrum" of Jewishness that has existed forever. At one end is the Jew who for whatever reasons doesn't even know that he is Jewish. At the other end is the ultra-Orthodox Jew who attempts to abide by the Torah and the 613 Laws every day of their lives. All Jews, whether they know it or not, sit somewhere on this spectrum in my opinion. As mentioned above, there is a Spark of the divine that exists in every Jew. The more that Spark is allowed to flourish, the more good things will be brought into the world. It's said that the whole purpose of the "agreement" between HASHEM and the Hebrews was to bring HASHEM, goodness, down into the physical world.

At 63 I began my trek back into Judaism from secularism even though I always felt "spiritual." There was no guide as to how to begin, what to watch out for, what to expect, or even where to start. I often wished there was some kind of "Judaism For Dummies" book out there but there was none. This is my attempt to provide one.

I was the ultimate Idiot Jew, a JINO, a Jew In Name Only, but I worked my way out of my idiocy. Now at my "advanced" physical age of 70 I'm still just a baby Jew, a newbie, a Jewbie. So undoubtedly there are "mistakes" concerning the religion of Judaism inside these covers that are quite obvious to those with more sophisticated knowledge. So what? Right or wrong, what's written is my truth of what I've learned up until now and if this book manages to bring even one other Idiot Jew out of their ignorance I will have succeeded, in spite of any internal errors.

Inside I explain generally, not specifically, where to start. I explain why you should be proud to be a Jew, what you've been missing out on, and how it will add to your life. I'll tell you things about Judaism that you've never heard before in your secular upbringing. It's fun, interesting, easy to read, and will make you say to yourself, "Hey, I want that!"

An Idiot Jew is the reality of who I was and who YOU are now. You're a Jew and you are an Idiot because you don't seek out your people by adding just a little bit of Jewish ritual into your life and therefore don't contribute to as much goodness in the world as you could. That pains you. In addition, you know intuitively that exploring and studying Judaism will enhance your life. Yet you still don't do it. Idiot Jew. Read this book!

Return To Judaism tells you not only where you might start but reinforces why you have the urge to start. Living in the world without a religious anchor means you exist in the "pit," where everything from "normal" people to deviant people are in your universe. Moving forward in your Judaism takes you out of the pit and into a place of like-minded people. It's not perfect there but it's safer, calmer, and, really, where you belong.

Is your family life a bit dysfunctional? Are you "socially drinking" or taking too many recreational or prescribed drugs? Are you not succeeding where you know you should be? You know something is missing inside and that things "should" and "could" be better. This book will bring you new perspectives to all these situations.

Becoming more religiously Jewish will help. A lot. It doesn't mean becoming obviously devout or praying three times a day. If you do, more power to you! Piety is not the goal here. Moving on the Jewish spectrum from nothing to something is the goal. Adding good things to your life is the aim and you don't have to give anything up. Negative things and negative people will simply molt away. Just by doing a few Jewish "things" will cause a change that will roll over your entire being. You'll see things differently. You'll dream differently. No one even has to know the changes you've made to your lifestyle.

Return To Judaism suggests easy ways to return to your roots: home, the place you feel happy and secure. You are one of the "Chosen People" (this book tells you what that actually means because nobody else has told you). Once you understand this, why would you want to block it? Embrace it. Just maybe it will change your life for the better!

I spent six decades as an Idiot Jew, secular, single, dating all religions, never going to synagogue. At the age of 61 I had sextuple bypass surgery (CABG-6). I went through it in a very cavalier fashion, never thinking anything could go wrong. And it didn't. I was very lucky. I never said a prayer, just assumed I'd be fine. I was. I knew my chest would be cracked open, my heart would be stopped and placed on a tray, and that the surgeon would then start sewing on it. Soon afterwards I realized, "Holy-Moly what did I put myself through?" If there was any time for prayer in my life, that was it! You're probably thinking, oh he had heart surgery so that brought him back to Judaism. No, the heart surgery didn't bring me back. I was a full-fledged Idiot Jew.

Amazingly, I did the whole surgery thing backwards from normal. Most people have a Primary doctor and a Cardiologist who then recommends a Surgeon. I had neither a Primary nor Cardiologist because I was always healthy. But I personally knew a heart surgeon at the time of my original stress situation so I called him for advice. The surgeon, located in another state, told me to travel up to his state immediately and he then set up appointments with Cardiologists he knew and trusted and got me seen right away. Things progressed in that backwards fashion. Like I said, it wasn't the operation that sent me back to Judaism.

When I returned home, I needed a Cardiologist for follow up care. A secular Jew who I knew recommended one to me. I liked the Cardiologist a lot. The doctor wore a yarmulke on his head while examining me. At first it seemed more odd than comforting, but I really didn't care either way. The doctor, obviously an Orthodox Jew, never offered any religious comments or suggestions, I guess because he didn't know for sure that I was Jewish as I had legally changed my last name from Apfelbaum (obviously Jewish) to Harvey (probably not Jewish). Or perhaps his level of observance didn't allow for any Jewish comments or suggestions in the office. I still don't know why he never brought up the topic of Judaism.

So after two years of seeing him regularly after my open heart operation and for no reason at all (uh huh), I suddenly and inexplicably asked him, "What's the best way for me to get back, get started, in Judaism."

His eyes lit up as I had never seen before and he said, "You HAVE to attend an 'outreach Shabbat service' held every Friday night at my Orthodox Temple."

"Doc," I said, "I'm not Orthodox and I don't speak any Hebrew."

He responded, "You HAVE to try it once. The service is held in a basement classroom, everyone attending are also beginners, it's mostly in English, and the Rabbi is a friend of mine, a good guy, young, knowledgeable, and very funny."

So, by chance (or was it?), at age 63, I went to a beginner Shabbat service in the basement of the Orthodox Synagogue and decided that for some reason I actually felt pretty good afterwards. That was my first baby step back home. The service was light and easy, exactly one hour long (so I never felt trapped or itchy for the end), mostly English except for a few prayers, some singing, and lots of jokes and humor. I kept going, not weekly at first, only once per month. Then I "automatically" found myself attending the services weekly, actually looking forward to Friday night. Now I rarely miss a Friday night service. Coming from my secular perspective I figured, "if it feels good, do it!" So, I did it.

Little by little my not-so-bad but not-so-good life changed. Now I'm imploring YOU not to wait until you are 63 years old. Life is short. Being Jewish is an honor, a privilege, and a responsibility, and is there for you to enjoy. HASHEM will delight in your effort. Remember this, HASHEM doesn't need you. You need Him.

So, this book explains many things that make it easy to find your way within the Jewish community that, surprisingly, doesn't make it so easy, especially for single people (read on for further explanation). Even if you take no action whatsoever this book will educate you about where you came from and allow you to see better the issues facing all Jews, religious and non-religious, of every denomination, around the world. Your perspective will change and with it the anchor of Judaism will enhance the rest of your life.

And there's one last thing I should mention. I sought no recommendations from Jewish organizations or Rabbis about the contents within these pages. After all, with chapters like "The Idiot Jew" and "Idiot Rabbis" it doesn't immediately lend itself to endorsements. I purposely wanted to keep the contents expressed from a beginner point of view including all the mistakes of a Jewbie. But even so, Return To Judaism is the perfect "leave behind" by any Rabbi officiating an event, or gift for a layperson to give to someone they know is secular and yearning for more. And in doing so they just might bring a few non-religious Jews back into the fold. I'm told it's a magnificent merit!

Have fun. Do good.

CHAPTER I

The Idiot Jew

How it's possible to reclaim goodness in your life

Let me state unequivocally that I am the biggest, baddest, broadest Idiot Jew on the planet. I'm #1, I'm #1, I'm #1!

My bone fides are that I spent OVER six decades as a secular Jew. How stupid is that? It's like people who state on dating websites, "I'm spiritual but not religious." They proudly announce to the world that they know for certain that there is a God but they do absolutely nothing, all day, every day, to connect to Him. As if, I know that there is something really good there but I'm too lazy to reach for it or make any effort to grasp it. Oh, that's really attractive.

But in some ways it's not really their fault. They were raised that way, as was I. But it can change. It can be reversed. You CAN choose a path to good things in your life. Just don't wait 63 years to do it like I did.

Being an Idiot Jew is, and is not, the fault of your parents.

In their time, assimilation into American life was a matter of survival. Later, in the next generation, it became the goal of parents for their children and of the children themselves to be socially popular rather than religious. Both didn't want to have any anti-Jew bias affect their social success. And also, it was so much "easier" just to light Chanukah candles around Christmas time when everybody else was enjoying the holiday spirit and then do nothing else.

The intention of assimilation into the American way of life was good. But now it's apparent that those seeking assimilation in the recent past sloughed off way too much, going overboard, and by doing so actually robbed many present-day Jews of the birthright they know for certain lives inside them.

The definition of the Idiot Jew IS the secular Jew. He has been "chosen" by HASHEM but is too "busy" to respond in kind. Busy, busy, busy, everyone is busy. The secular Jew is involved in learning, running a business, building a family, and going after all the pleasures life affords them. Generally, they are proud they are Jews. They light candles on Chanukah and attend synagogue on the High Holy days. That's their "duty" as a Jew. Some don't even do that! Idiots.

That was me.

My grandfather came from Germany in the early 1900's. He was an Orthodox Jew and spoke only Hebrew and Yiddish. I don't know what experiences my grandfather lived through but my father, the oldest of five children, was really big into American assimilation: Mother, baseball, and apple pie. His siblings, my three uncles and one aunt were the same way. They all spoke English and although they all had different levels of Jewish observance none maintained an Orthodox or even a kosher household.

My dad often spoke of changing our last name from Apfelbaum to Appel or some other iteration. He didn't like that a name ending in "baum" was a signal to the world that we were Jewish. But he never did change it. I did. When I was in my early 20's I legally reversed my middle and last names from Michael Harvey Apfelbaum to Michael Apfelbaum Harvey. He never told me not to change my name but I sensed that he wasn't happy about it either. I was the product of how he raised me. 80 years ago in America anti-Semitism was somewhat of a real fear and danger, but during my lifetime it hasn't been at all.

My two older sisters did not have a Bat Mitzvah and I wouldn't have had a Bar Mitzvah either except there was my Orthodox grandfather. I think my father's plan A was that his father would pass on prior to my 13th birthday. But he didn't and so plan A went out the window. As I hadn't been attending Hebrew school this was a huge problem. How can an Orthodox Jew have a grandson who doesn't have a Bar Mitzvah?

Plan B involved a conversation with the Rabbi at my grandfather's Orthodox synagogue. He suggested that there were only a couple of days throughout the year when a Bar Mitzvah is permitted to occur on a Sunday instead of a Saturday. One of those days was four days after my birthday and luckily appropriate for me. Instead of reading a Torah portion in Hebrew as is normal for a Saturday Bar Mitzvah, on Sunday you only had to chant several lines of the Haftorah.

Believe it or not, there existed an LP vinyl record available that contained those chants. One of my uncles who maintained his fluency in Hebrew got together with me weekly and helped me memorize those few chants phonetically. He stood with me on the Bima (the place where the Torah scroll is read to the congregation) and when the Rabbi signaled to my uncle that it was time for me to chant the verses, he would give me a little kick on the leg and away I would go. All went well, except not so much.

Afterward, my grandfather came up to me in the back of the synagogue to congratulate me with a smile and a handshake. I didn't speak Hebrew or Yiddish and he didn't speak English. My uncle translated. There seemed to be some kind of animated discussion going on between the two of them and my uncle didn't seem to be too happy.

Apparently the "teacher" of the Bar Mitzvah boy is supposed to be in attendance on the special Bar Mitzvah day. My grandfather was asking where my teacher was. Since neither my uncle nor my dad was aware of this little detail of Jewish Orthodoxy my uncle quickly answered that my teacher was on vacation in Florida. It was a lie to his father that he was not happy to tell.

So, the attempt of my father to "honor thy father and mother" with all good intentions was not as pure as it should have been. Having the Rabbi in on the little deceit didn't raise my level of respect for religion in general and Judaism specifically. And as I grew older it impacted my growth into an opinion that religion was a fraud and not so meaningful. This was another nail in the coffin that proved secularism was more real. I didn't fool the Rabbi. I don't think I fooled my grandfather. And I certainly didn't fool HASHEM.

In Judaism a boy becomes responsible for his sins after his 13th birthday. Prior to that it's his father's sin. So, exactly, whose sin was it?

As a thirteen-year-old who was crazy about playing all sports, this little sham was a trifecta of indolence. I didn't have to go to Hebrew school. I got through the Bar Mitzvah. And there was a little party afterwards with gifts. So, at the time I was fine with the whole deal…now, not so much.

However, when I look around at some of the "Bar Mitzvahs" I see today it certainly doesn't rank as the least holy, by far. After all, it did take place in an Orthodox Synagogue, I did recite the verses quite well even though I didn't have a clue as to what I was saying, and I did receive the Bar Mitzvah boy energy contained in the room.

Secular life in my family involved lighting the candles on Chanukah and we had an annual family Seder that often included uncles. That was it. I never saw Shabbat candles lit, ever. Even though there was a Temple right across the street from our housing development in Roslyn, New York, we never attended. I remember walking through the Temple parking lot for years in order to get to the Little League baseball fields I used to play on. And every day for the 18 years I lived in that house we would pass right by that synagogue in order to get home. Our family never stepped through the door. What a lost opportunity!

Roslyn was a mostly Jewish community so I was meeting Jewish girls. However, I received an athletic scholarship in Tennis to attend a private prep school in New Jersey, Blair Academy. We applied to many schools and my dad would always ask for an attendance book whenever we arrived. He would then look down the list of names to figure out if there were enough Jews at the school for me (or him) to feel comfortable. At Blair there were enough for his satisfaction. So my dad protected me from being an outcast by rejecting all gentile schools, and he obviously had Jewish pride but as far as any Jewish education…fuggedaboutit.

At the time, late 60's, all prep schools had compulsory, nondenominational, religious services. At Blair I attended church on 5 days of the week for a total of 3 hours per week. You weren't expected to participate if you didn't want to but you were expected to be respectfully quiet. Many of us would sneak in books to read. Again, because about a third of the congregation (Jews) ignored the Pastor by reading or falling asleep, my respect for religion continued to be stunted and further reinforced secularism.

Blair was a male-only boarding school. No girls. I attended Columbia for a year and a half and dated an old Jewish girlfriend from Roslyn. Then I attended Bard College in upstate New York, met and married a secular gentile woman, and was divorced two years later at the age of 25. Then I moved to Atlanta for 22 years where I dated both Jewish and non-Jewish women, all secular.

Somewhere in this time frame I came to the stupid secular conclusion that I would no longer date Jewish women. I had had enough. It seemed to me at the time that the demands they made were not in proper proportion to what they were providing in the relationship. If both people are giving 60% into the relationship, then you have a surplus. If one person gives 60% and the other person gives 30% then there is always a lack in the relationship even though one person is giving more than would normally be expected. In this situation something has to give and usually it's the one giving the most and getting the least who bolts. And suddenly the one giving less than they should is stunned at their "loss." "Oh, please, don't leave me!" But by then it's too late.

Unfortunately, what I just described is the JAP syndrome, Jewish American Princess for those who don't know. And, by the way, now there are also Jewish American Princes. You can't blame them. It's how they were raised. No matter how homely a Jewish girl (or guy) may be, she is always the apple of her Jewish daddy's eye. She can do no wrong. She is as beautiful as any girl can possibly be. And she is raised believing that she deserves everything the world has to offer. It's a big job for any conscientious Jewish man to succeed in.

So that was my quagmire. I just couldn't take it anymore. I consciously and deliberately stopped dating Jewish women.

The really stupid part was that it never occurred to me that I only needed to find ONE good one and if I had stayed persistent it's likely I could have found her. So not only was I an Idiot Jew, but also a stupid Idiot Jew.

And ladies, how can you tell a Jewish American Prince? Narcissism. It's all about him. He stays attached to his mommy's pocketbook way longer than is appropriate. He's always right, never wrong. He's late a lot, with understandable excuses, from 5 minutes to an hour and will sometimes cancel altogether at the last minute. His life is more important than yours.

And there's one thing more I'd like to say, painting in broad brushstrokes, about non-Jewish women. Since they are not raised as Princesses they work very hard at relationships, are very kind, giving, and loving. However, once they are done with you, they are done with you. Jewish women are extremely devoted and loyal and do everything they can to keep a relationship alive even though they may be totally blind to their Princess-hood.

So that was my life of 63 years fully immersed in secular Jewish idiocy. Now you are probably thinking that since I added more religion into my life, I've since met the woman of my dreams. That hasn't happened. Sorry, it doesn't work like that. Putting more religion into your life is not a quid pro quo. You don't do something expecting a direct return. If you enter your study of Judaism with that attitude it's likely you'll be disappointed. Just do your study of Judaism and take what comes down the pike. Your life will be enhanced in ways you can't possibly anticipate.

The one main benefit of all religions is the community it inspires and creates. If no one knows you no one can celebrate your good times or commiserate with you during your difficult times. You can check the Yellow Pages or Yelp for a Dentist as a secular person would do, but getting a recommendation from a fellow Jew about a Jewish Dentist might be a better way to go about it and it "keeps the money within the family" if you know what I mean.

Paying annual dues to the Temple and attending High Holy services once per year as many Idiot Jews do to stay somewhat connected to Judaism (and covers your bases in case you actually do meet HASHEM in the hereafter), does not fully connect you with the community. A good way to move away from being an Idiot Jew is to invest in something that the synagogue is involved in at least once per month. This will connect you with the community. You can offer some time doing charity work, go to a lecture, or even just light candles every Friday night at sundown. Do you know that lighting candles is so easy to do?

Lighting candles is a long-standing tradition done by Jewish females all around the world. If no females are present then men are permitted to do it. When a woman lights candles at sundown they know that all Jewish women within their time zone all around the world are doing the same thing. Now that's what you call a connection!

You don't have to say the Sabbath prayer but it's so short and easy to memorize. You can learn it phonetically and the English translation is almost always provided. Then for the next hour or two while the candle is burning, every time you look at it you consciously and unconsciously continue the connection with your Jewish sisters. It's something you will look forward to every Friday night, whether you go bar hopping afterward or not. You can have your cake and eat it too! By performing this one simple act you become less of an Idiot Jew.

CHAPTER II

Why Pursue Judaism?

You say you are "spiritual" but not "religious." So the question of why you should pursue Judaism is mostly already answered. You feel and know that HASHEM is within you. That's the major part. So now you just have to get up and do some simple things that draw you closer.

You're a JINO, a Jew In Name Only. Describing yourself as spiritual but not religious you're announcing to the world that it's good to be "holy" but bad to be a "Holy-Roller." But inside you are yearning for more. Get over the Holy-Roller image. You'll never be a Bible-thumping Holy-Roller speaking in tongues or only in scriptural verses. Jews don't do the Holy-Roller thing. Jews do good things. But you can exercise the spiritual nature within you and as a result *your* life will improve immensely.

I'm not here to talk you into it. I'm here to show you how I increased Judaism in my life and show you how you can also, comfortably, receive benefits to your current secular lifestyle.

You won't be giving up much and you will be gaining quite a bit. You already feel the hunger for HASHEM. You just have to take the first step to eat from the spread that's already laid out for you.

The Idiot Jew as described here is defined as someone who was raised non-religious, secular, 10 to 90 years old. Those who are married live in non-religious homes of their own making and those who are single are completely lost. Other than the fact that they know they are Jewish they do nothing to water the seed within them. These Jews feel the spiritual essence but they just don't know what to do to make it happen.

The main principle of Judaism is that doing good things in the world brings the Spirit of the Creator, HASHEM, down into the physical world. Can't you do good things? Studying the Torah enables you to do good things. But you don't even have to study the Torah. Just study the 10 Commandments (that IS studying Torah!). You can do that can't you? Just doing that brings HASHEM down into the physical world.

The divine Spark that is in the Jew is a seed ready to sprout. Today there are so many Jews that walk around feeling that Spark, that seed ready to sprout, but have no idea how to water it and make it take root. So they don't. But just by taking baby steps it will take root.

What exactly is the benefit of adding a little religious practice into your life? Will you be richer, healthier, happier, or smarter? Maybe yes but not necessarily. Just because you do a good deed does not automatically mean that good fortune will come your way because of it. A Jew does a good deed because Jews do good deeds. That's the end of it. If you feel good about yourself after doing a good deed, well, fine then. That might add some depth to your mundane life.

But just know this. The Head Rabbi of the United Kingdom, Jonathan Sacks, left the terrestrial plain dying of cancer at 72 years of age. He lived his life in as devout a way as anyone, day after day. He did good things constantly and influenced many people with his wisdom and many people prayed for his recovery. Yet with all that he still died at a relatively young age. Doing good deeds in the world does not guarantee longevity, riches, or anything tangible. You don't do one in order to gain another. Judaism just doesn't work that way so don't ever take that expectation into your practice.

Since Judaism brings HASHEM down into the physical world doing mitzvahs, good deeds, does exactly that. Maybe there is some kind of "merit" in there for you on Judgment Day but in studying Judaism you'll discover that there seems to be no mention of any kind of Judgment Day. So, who knows exactly what is to be gained by doing mitzvahs. Why not just do them anyway without any expectation of reward? That's the whole point. Yes, "random acts of kindness" (often anonymous) brings HASHEM into the physical world.

HASHEM has provided the Ten Commandments and the Torah for you, not for Him. Take it or leave it. It's your choice whether to live according to those suggestions or not.

HASHEM gave you free will. Imagine that! What a generous gift! Will you accept it or not?

Here are just a few things that are likely to happen as you increase your Jewish observance level:

- The way you perceive the world will change.
- The way you act in the world will change.
- The people in your life will change for the better.
- The likelihood of meeting an appropriate mate increases.
- Your community of associations will widen.
- Your recreational activities will become purer.
- Your relationship with your parents will be more positive.
- Your relationship with your children and/or siblings will improve.
- The respect that your family and friends hold for you will increase.

All this is a good thing and happens without naming Judaism as the cause. People may know that you have increased your Jewish learning because they see you doing things like going to classes or attending services. But you never mention it as the reason *your* life has changed and never even mention that your life *has* changed. But they will see a change in you toward the positive. You'll smile more and be fun to be around.

In conversation you might say something like, "Well, from the Jewish perspective they say…" or "Biblically it says…" or "According to Jewish tradition that issue would be decided by…." But you never attach any expectation that others will see it that way. It's just as you see it. They can either consider your statement/solution or not. If they do consider it and find it reasonable/rational/sensible, although maybe not the easiest course of action, they could discover that Judaism might hold something valuable for them as well.

One of the facets of Judaism is that Jews don't proselytize. Either you are in or you want in of your own accord. No one is going to go out and try to bring you in. If you aren't self-motivated to learn more than you already know about Judaism then forget it. Don't think the red carpet will be thrown out to welcome you. Everyone, especially the Rabbis, are happy to see you and hope they see you again. But ultimately it's *your* effort that wins the day. I'm laying things out for you here. You can become less of an Idiot Jew if you want, I'm not going to twist your arm or talk you into it.

In many places within the Torah it implies that each Jew must come to Judaism from within his own core. You saw the front cover of this book "Return To Judaism" and it's subtitle "A Starting Point For Non-Religious Jews." You picked it up because, as a non-religious Jew, you were curious. The spark inside you responded and you picked it up. It's now up to you to read on and decide on your own if you are going to follow up or not. I'm suggesting here that there is a smarter way to live your life, but you are the one who has to make the effort. This book will help you get started but after that it's totally up to you.

It's said that Rabbis are required to reject a non-Jew coming to them to convert to Judaism not once but two times. It's common for them to turn converts away. A certain minimum level of motivation needs to be proven before a Rabbi accepts someone into study for conversion. After all, the Rabbi doesn't want to invest in the education of someone if it's just a passing fancy. You are already a Jew, not a non-Jew convert, but it's the same idea. It's essential that you supply the juice, jewce.

Just as an aside, it could be said that Chabad proselytizes because they go out all over the world and set up centers where Jews can increase their learning and/or observance. But they clearly don't proselytize because other than "finding" or "discovering" Jews who were unaware that they were Jews, their only "purpose" is to be "available" to non-religious Jews who feel, *on their own*, that they would like to further pursue their understanding. There is never any arm-twisting by Chabad Rabbis and there is definitely never any "outreach" to non-Jews for conversions.

Now listen. You can take up golf or chess or the piano or go to museums to enhance your life. But anything you take up to improve your appreciation of life and this Creation always seems to have a ceiling. You can only get so good at golf or chess or piano and you can visit every museum in the world. But when it comes to Judaism there is no ceiling…or, better said, the ceiling is Heaven.

There is no doubt that Judaism is a very high mountain to climb. And you shouldn't try to rip the skin off the snake. Take in as much as you feel comfortable taking in. I started by attending only one class for only one hour each week. C'mon you watch more TV than that!

Guess what? You meet new people in that class. These people are not looking to get you drunk and take your clothes off, or find out if there is a stream of money gushing into your bank account. They are there because they are pretty much done with drama, seeking deeper meaning to their lives. And so are you.

In my first class there were not one but two women who, when discussing the issue at hand, demonstrated remarkably clear, rational, and intricate thinking. You like "smart" in a woman? That's where smart is located. You also begin relating to a Rabbi, someone who is not perfect but who lives by a moral code. How many of your current friends consciously live by a moral code other than "if it feels good, do it?"

After attending class a few times, I decided I'd like to try services. I went to a "beginner" Shabbat service only just once per month. Beginner services are out there if you just look for them. The one I attended was an "outreach" service in a basement classroom at a local Orthodox synagogue. I knew no one. 40 to 60 people attended, mostly older than myself, and many were in my own newbie, Jewbie, position. Most didn't speak Hebrew and, like me, they would never attend a real Orthodox service. But they also felt the calling to "observe" within their own comfort level of understanding. None of us *ever* thought we'd be trudging into an Orthodox Jewish edifice on Friday nights, even though it was through the back door and down into the basement. But there we were, doing just that!

The Rabbi was young, energetic, and humorous. The service was mostly in English. He spent time talking about the doings of the local Jewish community, telling us of opportunities for charity work, attending multi-denominational (Jewish) holiday services, he told a joke weekly, and briefly touched on the "Parsha," that week's chapter of the Torah. So immediately, by attending services, you learn that there *is* a weekly lesson read every Saturday morning in the Synagogue. It's likely you didn't know that. Now you might become curious as to what those portions relate. I did and explored them further. All of a sudden I was "studying Torah." No one told me to do it. It just happened.

Also, at the service we would sing a little bit, in Hebrew with transliteration, and said some prayers also in Hebrew with transliteration. So there you are, speaking to HASHEM in the same language that Moses spoke to HASHEM 2,500 years ago. It definitely connects you. It changes you.

After these services I always felt "good." In what way, I

couldn't really put my finger on. What do you know? I began attending every week. Now I rarely miss a Shabbat service.

Although I never fully integrated socially with the group, because most were married couples, everyone became fond of each other. The Rabbi was always available to recommend a book or a business professional if needed, all within the Orthodox community. Again, no one is perfect but I actually like seeing my doctor, or lawyer, or some other professional person wearing a yarmulke. It just adds another level of security for me. HASHEM lives within that doctor, lawyer, or professional person. Although I wasn't fully in the community, I still felt like I was part of a community that could and would help me. This added to my previously secular life.

The Rabbi would share or recommend potent and interesting books to read. I started with "A Crash Course in Judaism," "The Rebbe," and "Jew vs. Jew." But you can start anywhere you want. Just get started. This is also "Torah study."

Jew vs. Jew was about how a Jewish community in New Jersey was formed and the way in which it grew and changed. It gave perspectives on how the three denominations of Judaism formed in their own natural way. Having grown up on Long Island, which is similar in culture to New Jersey, I was able to relate to a lot of it. Jews fight. They are stiff necked. It's good and it's bad. We're human.

The Rebbe seemed like a tome when I picked it up but it was actually pretty easy reading. It's a biography of a truly great man, a Jew who will make you proud to be a Jew. His intellectual capacity was off the charts amazing. What he did with his life was instructional and inspiring. It didn't send me off to buying a black suit, white shirt, and black hat. But it did reinforce my "feeling" for Judaism that I was on a really good path "hanging" with some really remarkable people.

Within the first three months of my first incursion back into Judaism I began a new early morning routine of coffee, a cookie, and one hour of reading. It set me up for my entire day as I connected with HASHEM in my own little way.

Then I found myself going to sleep a little earlier at night so that when I got up early to read, I'd be refreshed with a good night's sleep. This was a lifestyle change that came about organically. Yours will probably be somewhat different but for sure the days of waking up with a hangover will probably be gone! Is that such a bad thing?

Just allow things to grow on you as they come. HASHEM is with you in this process. Don't force it. As you grow morally you will find many things more challenging and many things easily decided upon. It's OK. You'll make a few Jewbie "mistakes." Don't worry about it. Let it happen. And don't make any goals, because doing so from your limited, still mostly secular awareness, might limit the eventual outcome of your efforts.

You probably won't become Orthodox so don't let that scare you. However, in my limited experience I know of four situations, three married couples and one single person, who did choose to become Orthodox after making the decision to leave secularism in their twenties.

One became a Rabbi and he and his wife had many children, some of whom became Rabbis as well. Another couple from Long Island made the Orthodox choice in their twenties, had five children in eight years, and eventually divorced which is kind of rare within the Orthodox community. Nevertheless, they are both happy and civil with each other, and all the children are Orthodox in observance and living physically and emotionally healthy lives.

The third couple, basic New York City urbanites, now reside in suburbia within walking distance of their synagogue, have the "normal" number of offspring, are healthy and successful in every way. He is an officer of their Orthodox Synagogue.

The single guy is an Israeli, was secular into his 30's, and became Orthodox. His Orthodoxy estranged him from his sister, by her choice not his, and I would guess that he is sad about that.

I'm not sure HASHEM is so interested in your *level* of observance as much as he is interested in how your actions affect others around you. The more observant you are, the less likely you are to do bad things. But you don't have to be Orthodox to do mitzvahs or "gain favor" in the eyes of HASHEM. You can be observant through Conservative or Reform denominations or not even attend services at all.

The important thing is living the Ten Commandments. If you do just that it brings HASHEM down into the physical world.

I struggle everyday living in the secular world with a Biblical perspective. But I know that I've turned the corner on assimilation. Assimilation has buried more Jews than Hitler. You are one of them. But it's never too late to rise from the dead. Assimilation continues unabated. If writing this book pulls even one Idiot Jew away from secular assimilation, then it's all been worth it. And it hasn't been easy.

Although I was in a situation that allowed me the time to write, actually putting in the time, day after day, was not an easy process. I'm not a writer, I'm an athlete. Then there was the expense of the book, money I really couldn't afford, that I had no choice but to invest. But ultimately it's not my money. It's money HASHEM provided, I reasoned, even though it was scary every time I wrote a check.

Your life will also take unusual turns, some fun and rewarding, some pretty scary. But the mitzvahs you end up doing are exactly what HASHEM brought you into the world to do. What more can you ask of life than that? Take that first step. You have no idea how things will change and they will. You will be the reality TV show that you currently watch, except you will be much more interesting and invigorated by it. And the mitzvahs will not necessarily be big, but whatever they are they will be no less important.

Just by reading this book you have already embarked on

the road to HASHEM. Has it made you better or worse? It's the first baby step. It has probably made you just a smidgen better but definitely not worse. There's a lot more "better" ahead for you.

I could state the Ten Commandments for you, in their proper order (the order of which *is* significant). But I won't. Google it. Do your own search. It's *your* process. Memorize the Ten Commandments. There are only ten! Then do your best to live by them. Believe me, if I can do it, after 63 years of devotion to secular living, so can you!

CHAPTER III
More Reasons To Get Started

The last chapter told you why it's in your best interests to add some more religion into your life and this chapter will tell you exactly how to ease into it without distress.

This book is for those Jews who were brought up with no religion in their life, "I'm spiritual but not religious." As that's who I used to be I know that there are a lot of you out there. Idiot Jews. Secular. Many are single and can't figure out why They are single, and some are unhappily in intermarriages. Still others have married within the faith, raised non-religious children, and can't figure out why there is so much dysfunction in their homes.

Torah study provides answers and solutions. It's hard but it's also pretty simple. You'll understand that paradox when Judaism becomes infused into your existence. Just by starting to study Torah your worldview will begin to change.

You'll see things more from a "Biblical perspective" because you'll be drawing off the combined wisdom from 3,500 years of brilliant scholars examining the same interpersonal things you are struggling with today. There is nothing new in the world. Torah study is much different than exploring pop psychology or the most current trend du jour to move your life into more joyous realms.

Every chapter, paragraph, verse, and word of the Torah has been examined in every possible way over these thousands of years. So the Jews probably got some things right. I'm proud to be a Jew because of all this study and hand-me-down wisdom.

The Torah is comprised of five books but there are nineteen more that make up the "Old" Testament. And there are volumes and volumes and volumes of discussions, arguments, and commentaries on every aspect you can possibly imagine. And it all talks about morals, values, and laws that add to and strengthen civil society.

Don't you want to know what some of these morals, values, and laws are, even if you choose not to follow any of them? Don't you want your children to know what they are, or at least know that they exist and where they can find them?

But you've been away from Jewish religiosity your entire life. And the Jewish religion is such a massive mountain to climb. All true. But, however much you add Torah study and Jewish ritual into your lifestyle, the benefits quickly become cumulative.

What? It's so hard to light candles on Friday nights? You

can't go to a Jewish history or Torah class for an hour once per week or read a book, five pages at a time, written by a Rabbi? C'mon, what have you got to lose? The downside is small and the upside is enormous!

But you don't know how to pray or feel "funny" doing it? I can tell you this, when you go to the Synagogue people pray all around you. Even though I try, I'm still not sure if I'm any good at it. And maybe they aren't good at it either. Relax. HASHEM doesn't measure your observance level so much as your effort level, and also your capacity to do good things in the world. Making the effort to add a touch of Jewish ritual into your life increases that capacity.

I started with no help from anybody.

I wear no jewelry, not even a watch. But for some reason, ha-ha, I had been wearing a gold chain with a medal on it for at least 20 years. The medal displays the two tablets of the Ten Commandments. It had been handed down within my father's family for generations and the date on the backside was 1867. I was named after two Rabbi's from that time period, Michael and Harvey, but I'm unaware of who the first person was that owned it. So for many years it sat on my skin, close to my heart, just sitting there, having come through less observant family members straight into a secular, assimilated, Idiot Jew like me. Hmmmm.

So it hit me, the Ten Commandments would probably be a good place for me to start. Why not learn about them?

I was embarrassed that I could only name about six of them. (Right now, how many can you name?) There were only ten of them so I figured I should learn about them and follow them. It became clear that I hadn't been following many of them so well and some of them not at all. I'd always been "unscrupulously" honest (do not lie), never stole anything (do not steal), and never murdered anyone (do not murder) so I had three in my corner.

(Actually, when you begin to study the Ten Commandments they are really quite complex. When I used the term above "'unscrupulously' honest" I soon realized it was probably not the most accurate description because when you tell someone you won't be home when you know you will be home the description changes to "'mostly' honest" and mostly honest isn't honest at all. And "never" stole anything probably should have been "never stole anything of great value," as in taking sugar from a restaurant table is, actually, stealing. But my above descriptions came from a formerly "spiritual but not religious" framework.)

There is more written in the next chapter about the Ten Commandments but for now I'd like you to know that when I looked around and saw that most of the people I surrounded myself with also didn't live by the Ten Commandments, I was shocked even further. One of my sisters lives her life having broken nine of ten (there's still time for her to murder someone, but she would *never* do that because she's such a "good" secular person). And even from a secular perspective it was no wonder I wanted to have nothing to do with her.

Now look around at your own life. Who have you surrounded yourself with? Are they decent people? Do they follow the Ten Commandments? Having no guidepost secular people are really quite dangerous. For example, ask yourself this question, how many murderers on death row attended church on the Sunday prior to their crime? The answer is probably none (except for the guy who killed parishioners in a church on a Sunday, but you get my drift). The non-religious is one end of the spectrum.

The other end of the spectrum is the devout religious leader. Although there might be a rare exception, if you leave your wallet within easy reach of a devout religious leader it's likely it will remain undisturbed.

Even though you are secular or even a total atheist, you still exist, whether you like it or not, on a moral spectrum. If HASHEM (who you don't believe in) isn't judging you (and He is), many other people in this life will. You'll soon realize that if you do nothing more than increase people in your life who live more by the Ten Commandments than those that don't it stands to reason that your life will be less tumultuous.

Continuing on, the Adultery Commandment was the one that really got to me. As a successful Tennis Pro the ability to break this Commandment was a constant temptation. I felt awful having submitted to the temptation on three occasions. Within my newfound Biblical perspective the memory of the extreme pleasure of those acts soon transformed itself in my mind, not because I felt bad for the woman who had an equal part in the sin, but because I felt so bad for the man! Even if he were somewhat or even totally responsible for the crime, I shouldn't have committed it.

To this day, if I had to live my life over, this is the one "mulligan" I'd like to do over and I would now welcome another temptation just to prove my own ethical improvement. Adultery is a crime that is impossible to atone for or provide restitution for. I'll just have to rely on the forgiving nature of HASHEM. And what about the moral fiber of the woman who created the temptation? Is that the kind of woman I want to be surrounding myself with? Not anymore.

Coveting. What's wrong with that? My neighbor has a nice car, why shouldn't I want a nice car? This Commandment is not so much about committing a sin so much as it is about lowering the stress level in your life. Maybe you like stress and drama. I don't.

Life is full of opportunities to attain satisfaction on your own like hitting a perfect shot on the tennis court or golf course. Let your own life lead you to your own satisfactions. I'll leave this at that. As in everything else within Judaism there are deeper reasons for not coveting. Also note, this Commandment resides entirely in your thoughts, but actions are conceived in your thoughts.

So when you begin leading your life within the Ten Commandments things change and they change for the better. Not only being around good people lifts you up, but also people from strangers to long-time friends will see you differently. This will be good for you when different people enter your life. This affects you and will affect your family in a positive way even if they don't choose to follow the Ten Commandments as you do.

These five Commandments just elucidated deal with man's relationship with his fellow man and are contained in the second Tablet. They are pretty clear. Either you did the deed or you didn't. The first Tablet and the first five Commandments relate to man's relationship with HASHEM. Here each person has to measure on his own how deeply attached he is to his Creator. So now you know the distinction between the five Commandments on each side of the tablets. You're learning!

Although there are many subtleties to the first three commandments, believing in Monotheism, keeping no idols, and not taking HASHEM'S name in vain, they are mostly easy to abide by. Keeping the Sabbath and honoring your father and mother are more difficult.

I mentioned earlier a moral "spectrum" that exists even though some will deny that it does. There is also a "Jewish" spectrum. A Jew is a Jew is a Jew. There are all kinds. The strict definition is that if your mother was a Jew, whether secular or observant, then you are a Jew. Whether you like it or not and whether you are an Atheist or not you are on the Jewish spectrum. A looser definition of "Jew" contains those non-

Jews who convert and mixed religious families that follow the customs and rituals of the Jewish religion. Regardless, the Jewish spectrum runs from the secular Idiot Jew to the most observant.

Concerning the Sabbath, I had no idea what it actually was from a Biblical perspective. From the Secular perspective it was hey, it's Friday night, I can sleep late tomorrow, let's party. I discovered the Biblical perspective regarding the Sabbath was far more potent than just a night of joking around.

There are all different levels of keeping the Sabbath. My Reform Rabbi invited me to play golf on Saturday. A Conservative Rabbi probably would not play golf on Saturday and an Orthodox Rabbi would definitely not play golf on Saturday. So keeping the Sabbath for most Idiot Jews seems impossible at first, but at whatever level you observe it is quite rewarding.

Not using screens for 25 hours (the Sabbath day is one hour longer than 24) is actually revitalizing. So if you just can't stop watching TV on the Sabbath, at least give up the computer for a day. It will all still be there when you return.

If you have a family it's easy to do things to observe the Sabbath. Going to the beach, the park, or visiting neighbors weekly is great. Just being together as a family adds to your life. And what's wrong with eating a lot and napping a lot?

The Sabbath means that there is more spiritual energy in the world for 25 hours. (Again, see how much you are learning already!) The idea is to feel that energy and you can. You aren't supposed to drive on the Sabbath but if you drive to the beach or the park and you open yourself up to the spiritual energy, tapping into the creation of nature, I'm guessing HASHEM might forgive the "sin" of driving. Do what you feel comfortable with. Remember you're a Jewbie. As you become more observant your comfort and understanding level will advance.

Since many Idiot Jews are single keeping the Sabbath is a much bigger problem. Saturday used to be like every other day for me. I'd do business, do physical work, and generally treat it like every other day of the week. So I transformed it into a special, different day. My friends are my "family." There is a tennis doubles get together every Saturday amongst some tennis Pros where I live. We play and go out afterwards for beer and wings. That's my Sabbath.

That kind of Sabbath is probably just fine with the Reform but the Orthodox would say the activity is not even close to a Sabbath observance. But for me it becomes a special activity, a different day of the week, where I "feel" HASHEM and am relaxed and joyful. It definitely reorients my view of the past week and the future week. This is a good thing in my life even though it doesn't live up to the measure of the Orthodox.

If more devout Jews look mockingly at this, they can. That's the best I can do. On my Sabbath I also sleep late, read for more than an hour in the morning, meet with other friends for dinner. I drive my car. I set the cruise control at the speed limit and most cars just whiz past me. If those who are more devout laugh at my version of Sabbath, HASHEM understands. Remember, as a Jewbie the Sabbath is a "different" day. I get that there is more spiritual energy in the air and I try my best to breath the energy in. Regardless, by keeping "my" Sabbath I'm playing within the Ten Commandment "rules" and gain benefits (physical, emotional, and psychological) from it. Try it. You'll like it.

And finally, there's the Honor Your Mother and Father Commandment. Our parents took care of us when we were children. They might not even have liked or loved us (they probably did!). But they saw to it that they fed, clothed, and gave us a safe environment for at least two decades. So, too, this Commandment asks us to do the same for our parents. You don't have to love them or even like them but you do have to make sure they are clean, well fed, and safe for at least two decades. Plan on it and budget for it. Hopefully your siblings will share in the financial "burden."

My parents are deceased. So I'm "off the hook," right? I don't think so. This Commandment also relates to honoring those who are older and wiser than we, including authority figures. We should respect Vets, Police, Fireman, Clergy, Doctors, Nurses, and anyone who takes care of us. What about the aged with no family? Would it kill us to find one and visit? Who benefits more from this visitation, them or you?

So being more "religious" simply means reorganizing your

life in a way that you drop certain parts of your mundane, secular, lifestyle and add other parts that are not all that time consuming. You don't have to stop watching TV but watch a little less, do just a little less bar hopping, and spend your money just a touch differently. It's really not a big deal and it definitely pays off.

Are you getting the picture yet? Quoting scripture is not who you will become. You'll still be you except you'll be wiser, happier, and more attractive. You'll see solutions to problems in your life much quicker and with greater potency. Your solutions will not come back to bite you as many of your former decisions did. The more you understand as you study the more you will walk in a decent, relaxed fashion. If you get stuck a consultation with your Rabbi will "fix" it pretty quickly. There will be no need for years of expensive therapy.

It's all within your grasp right now. Get started in whatever fashion makes you comfortable. Judaism is a religion of obligation and responsibility. It teaches you that if you have a difficulty look to yourself for the solution. Don't expect someone else to make it better. I find this amazing. Judaism teaches you that YOU have the power. Your life is NOT dependent on others.

There is one aspect of Judaism that you probably don't know about. From earliest times there have been Jews who do nothing all day except study Torah. It's their occupation to do so and the community supports them in this effort. They are the ones who find new insights from the Torah in which to raise the morals and values of their community and the world. They exist even today. That's how important "Torah Study" is to Jewish life. Even if you don't do Torah study all day long, Torah study for whatever amount of time you put in is to your benefit.

Now I'm here to tell you that the little reading that you might do for just an hour a day in the morning IS Torah study! You don't have to open the Torah and study. You can open up a book *about* the Torah and you'll be *doing* Torah study. When you do this your secular perspective will begin to acknowledge a Biblical perspective. You'll begin to compare the two perspectives and decide which one is superior. That's when you become transformed. When you start asking yourself, "what can I do to improve my situation?" the answers will just pop right up because of your Torah study. Then it's your responsibility to act. No one can help you better than yourself. Do it or don't. It's up to you.

I recently encountered a secular person who posited the idea that a thief lives a better life than a non-thief. They live in nicer homes, drive nicer cars, have beautiful clothes and teeth, and travel all over the world. As long as you don't get caught and prosecuted and end up in jail, stealing pays. He was right! But stealing does not bring HASHEM down into the physical world. Torah study makes every life decision pretty obvious.

The obligation to study Torah that Judaism demands of the Jew is for YOU! HASHEM will be HASHEM whether you choose to take His gift or not. You can make it onerous or you can make it pleasurable. It's totally up to you.

Baby steps. Start now!

CHAPTER IV

ABRAHAM, MOSES, & THE TEN COMMANDMENTS

Most "spiritual but not religious" Idiot Jews know nothing about Abraham. I know this because for 63 years I didn't know anything about him. I knew about Moses, Jesus, Buddha, Rama, and Krishna. I knew about Washington, Lincoln, and Dr. King. I knew about Moe, Larry, & Curly, Martin & Lewis, and Abbott & Costello. I knew about Cher, Madonna, and Gaga. I knew that Abraham wasn't part of a male comedy act and I knew that he wasn't a single-named female singer. But did I know even one thing about Abraham? I knew his name but that was it.

I didn't know whether Abraham lived before or after Moses, or before or after Jesus. I certainly didn't know anything about what he did in life. How pathetic was that? And I'm certain that many other Idiot Jews out there right now are just as pathetic as I was. Most practicing Jews will probably find this level of ignorance hard to believe but it's very, very, ashamedly true.

Lack of knowledge is a terrible thing. Ignorance seems to be dominating the majority culture today in terms of general education. Compared to one hundred years ago eighth graders then knew more than High School graduates know now. But that's a different topic for another book (not authored by me!)

Keep in mind I was well traveled through coaching tennis on an international level, well-educated by northeastern prep schools and Ivy League colleges, and knew a lot of things about a lot of things. But Isaac, Jacob, and Joseph? Blank. At the age of 63 I knew less about Torah than a 5-year-old Orthodox child.

All I knew about Isaac was that it was the first name of a violinist virtuoso named Stern. All I knew about Joseph was that it was the first name of Stalin, a bad man. All I knew about Jacob was that it was the first name of my grandfather, a good man. What I missed out on in terms of wisdom was enormous because I was totally ignorant about any of my Jewish forefathers. But for now, let me tell you what I learned about Abraham that amazed me beyond belief. After becoming a little more educated in the Torah I couldn't fathom how information of this enormity about this great man escaped me.

Abraham was considered the very first "Jew." In his time they were called Hebrews. Now that I know a little bit about him, I take great pride in being a Jew, feeling close to a man who changed the course of history for the entire planet, Jews and non-Jews alike, from 3,500 years ago. His influence still goes on even today.

First of all, he is remembered as the very first monotheist at a time in history when the culture had thousands of gods: sun, moon, sea, earth, river, rain, you name it god. Abraham said, no, there is only one God who created all that is and rules over everything that is. What a concept! And he gained followers in this notion simply by being "kind." The culture was extremely violent and cruel at the time so being "kind" was mostly rare behavior.

He was kind in that his tent was set up with no walls and every passerby who wanted a place to stay and food to eat was invited in. He was such a nice, kind, caring man in such a vicious world that this alone brought him notoriety.

As if the notion of monotheism and kindness wasn't earth shattering enough, Abraham asked of his followers only two simple things: 1) do good, and 2) learn something new every day. This was pretty basic stuff but it changed the course of history especially in his time and also subsequently in our time. As a Jew it's nice to know that I'm one of him, or he's one of me, or something like that. And you can be one of him too!

As to #1 above, "do good," the Hebrews who stayed around Abraham posited the idea that in order to get to Heaven you simply had to "do good." So even if you believed in one of the other thousands of gods at the time a path to

Heaven, according to Abraham, existed for you just by doing good deeds. This Jewish theology still exists today.

Without being critical of Christians, they say you can *only* reach Heaven if you "accept" Christ into your life. Without being critical of Muslims, they say you can *only* reach Heaven if you "obey" Allah. Jews say, "do good" and you'll get to Heaven. So if you are an Aborigine in Australia and never heard of Christ or Allah there is no theological path for you to get to Heaven. That doesn't seem quite fair. But Jews believe that the same Aborigine in Australia who never heard of Abraham or Moses or the Ten Commandments *can* attain Heaven just by doing good deeds. Even atheists and agnostics can attain Heaven according to Jewish theology by doing good deeds in the world. Thanks Abraham!

As to #2 above, "learn something new every day," Abraham changed the course of human history by suggesting that people learn one new thing every day. Pretty simple yet earth shattering. At his time in history humans were locked into linear cultural evolution, meaning that whatever occupation your father did you also did, over and over, generation after generation. There was no need or reason to know or learn anything else.

If you were a rich royal, you lived a rich life. If you were a poor beggar, you begged. If you were a shoemaker's son you made shoes, a farmer's daughter you farmed. There was no freedom to move into any other lifestyle to improve your living situation. There were no trade schools or schools of any kind and there was no desire anywhere within the culture to add to one's knowledge base. Upward mobility was not a concept in existence.

By suggesting that you "learn something new every day" the natural human capacity to gain knowledge increased in the world, little by little, through the Jews. For example, a Hebrew sheepherder would take the time to herd his sheep and also learn about astronomy, one new fact every day. By doing so, through time, he became an expert in astronomy and then had the capacity to become a navigator and break away from his father's sheepherding occupation if he so desired.

A farmer would also learn mathematics, one new idea each day, and would gain the capacity to become a money manager. And on and on so the Hebrews became very adept at many different disciplines. All of a sudden human evolution became non-linear, open to whatever creative genius might occur. This was completely new in the world then and is still applicable to today. Thanks Abraham!

It's quite obvious that this critical objective of daily education still exists as a key ingredient to advancement and success. Look at how hard Asians and students from India work in school. In contrast, look at the culture of present inner-city schools in America where getting good grades are looked down upon by the existing majority. Lowering standards to allow matriculation regardless of skills is the brilliant solution of adults in decision making positions. Those poor people are locked into a primitive linear evolution of their own making. Stuck. They are in poverty for generation after generation. It's not a matter of race and it's not a matter of poor teachers or resources. It's a matter of how parents, and/or elders, in the community instill the Abrahamic idea of learning something new every day.

Hebrews began advancing in many ways beyond the average culture surrounding them. And as such they benefited the societies within which they lived because they were making advancements in agriculture, husbandry, astronomy, and much more. And all this that I'm describing is without any discussion of the values and morals that would naturally devolve from these two, simple, Abrahamic "demands."

Now, when I discovered what an incredible impact Abraham had, *and is still having on the world 3,500 years later*, I realized maybe there is more to this Jewish thing than just being "spiritual" without being "religious." I figured maybe I should just live according to the Ten Commandments "allegedly" given to Moses by HASHEM to the Hebrews at Mount Sinai after leaving Egypt 1,000 years after Abraham.

Now Moses is considered in Jewish tradition to be the greatest of all prophets. He was the only one who spoke directly to HASHEM. The other prophets received their inspiration in other indirect ways. Moses was the intermediary when HASHEM chose to speak to the entire nation of Hebrews. HASHEM didn't just choose to speak to a few lucky ones but he spoke to the whole group. Although Moses didn't write the Ten Commandments he delivered them, twice (the first time he smashed them due to celebrations around the golden calf and the second time in order to replace the first ones). They were written on the tablets by HASHEM. Moses was also the one who delivered the Torah.

It was Moses who confronted the Pharaoh and was the one who led the Jews to freedom by carrying out HASHEM'S plans. He brought into the physical world miracle after miracle after miracle, so many miracles. Moses wasn't a high-tech genius, political activist, or fame chasing personality. In fact, he argued with HASHEM on many occasions about being the one to carry out His plans. But he managed the best he could and has been revered by Jews through time for his place in history. In his own way Moses was just as essential to the human condition as Abraham was.

So to me the Ten Commandments seemed simple enough. Thankfully there weren't twenty! But if you really think about it, would you add or subtract one or two Commandments or are the ten totally complete? What would you add that's not already morally covered? What would you subtract? The values and morals contained there in the Ten, according to Jewish tradition, are simply and totally complete.

Soon I discovered the Ten Commandments were not so easy after all as they contained hidden depth. Ridiculously and firstly, I realized I couldn't even name all Ten Commandments. Can you? I remembered only four, part of the second tablet that suggests how man should treat his fellow man.

How pathetic! And I called myself a Jew? Oh, yeah, but I'm "spiritual."

I got: don't lie, don't steal, don't commit adultery, and don't kill (which I later learned that the Hebrew word translates into "murder," not "kill" because in self-defense HASHEM permits us to kill). The one in the second tablet that I missed was to not covet. What's wrong with coveting? My neighbor has a big house so I want a big house. But if you begin to examine all the things that you covet, which is mostly everything that exists on the planet, it will drive you crazy.

You simply can't do everything there is to do on Earth. There are too many nations to experience, too many museums to visit, too many beaches, mountaintops, sports and music to enjoy. By not coveting I discovered that both my mind and body began to relax. That's a good thing.

Then I read through the five Commandments on the first tablet, the ones that suggest how man should relate to HASHEM. I had heard them all before but since I avoided being "religious" I just couldn't remember them. Honor your Father and Mother was simple enough. Just a little religiosity taught me that I didn't necessarily have to love them, just don't let them starve on the street. Keep them clean, clothed, and fed. They did the same for you for a couple of decades after you were born so you can return the favor.

Sorry, not done there with the Father and Mother thing. This Commandment, I discovered, also refers to *all* people *older* than you. It has to do with honoring and respecting authority figures, something that is sadly lacking in our culture today. Police are insulted and disregarded. Teachers are disobeyed. Parents are cursed at (the penalty for cursing at your parents within the Jewish tradition is death, so the emphasis as to how bad a thing this is becomes obvious although there is no recorded incident that this penalty was ever carried out). This lack of respect throughout our culture today is a sign of a declining society and not a pleasant notion to realize.

However, within religious communities disobeying this Commandment is not tolerated. And so those communities are peaceful and well regulated. In comparison, secular cities today are in total chaos with no hope of getting better.

Number 1 of the Ten Commandments is the best one of all. "Thou shall have no other Gods before me." Of course, easy, I'm already "spiritual" and "believe." Yeah, you think so but not so fast. Upon further study you find out that you have to love your God with all your heart and all your soul. That's the kicker. I mean you really, really, really have to love HASHEM.

It turns out it's not so easy to do. You can say you love Him with all your heart and all your soul on Monday and then on Tuesday realize you didn't. This conundrum will never end because you can always love HASHEM *even more*. But the act of loving HASHEM even more every day changes you and changes the world. Checkmate.

Number 2 is also a piece of cake, so you think. "Do not worship idols." The difficulty becomes the definition of the word "idols." It's not only woodcarvings of the sun attached to a wall that's considered an idol. The belief that crystals (rocks) have healing power or posters of Marilyn Monroe or any other pop icon is the ultimate Heaven to be striven for is ludicrous.

Idols can also be gobs of money, executing political power, seeking physical beauty, and even family pride can be an idol. Just be careful, that's all. There are many things to pursue in life but remember HASHEM is the one and only and there is no physical symbol, place, or being that can contain Him.

With Abraham, Moses, and the Ten Commandments on your team how could you not want to be a Jew fan? It's a greater place of attachment than a Yankee fan for sure.

You don't have to wait to be drafted onto the team, traded there, or acquired as a free agent. You just have to show up, participate in workouts, and hone your skills. The team is waiting for you. You just have to make the choice. Start easy so you don't pull a muscle and work your way into shape. Hello! Choice made yet?

CHAPTER V

The Three Denominations of Judaism

I'm just a baby Jew, a newbie, a Jewbie. I started exploring Judaism at 63 years old. As I write this, I'm 70. So, in 8 years of discovery I'm hardly an expert on Judaism. Many people more knowledgeable than I would probably dispute some of the things I've written in this book. That's OK. I'm writing to a "beginner" audience. All I'm doing is reporting my "impressions" of what I've learned over the short period of my study, accurate or inaccurate. Admittedly some of those impressions may be wrong. The goal here is to hook up with other beginners in a way that supports them in knowing that they aren't alone out there and that they can get involved in Judaism painlessly.

I'm addressing Jews who know very little or nothing at all so I'm attempting to give them a big picture, from my point of view, of the various worlds of Judaism. If they choose to get started, at least they will know the basics and allow them to pick their own "spots" more appropriately. So please, forgive any forthcoming inaccuracies.

What most non-religious Jews don't realize is how unique the religion is to other world religions. Yes, we have holidays and rituals like other religions but we don't idolize wise "men" in human form or objects, animate and inanimate, in Nature. Wise men are wise men but not the Creator. Even Nature is small in comparison to the Creator. In Judaism the Creator, HASHEM, is worshiped and the one to whom we pray. This idea is older than other religions and still revered today.

In Jewish history there have been many prophets. Some we know of and some we don't. Prophets would hear the word of HASHEM in various ways such as dreams or instantaneous inspiration. The Torah claims that Moses was the greatest of all prophets because he had the capacity to speak directly to HASHEM on many occasions. And Abraham is also considered a great prophet for all the morals and values he elucidated that advanced and continues to advance the human condition. But both of these great "men," two prophets of many, though honored and revered, are viewed in their proper place and are not worshiped as gods.

And while we are on the topic of men it would be helpful at this point to address women in Judaism. Many women are turned off to Judaism because they have the impression that women are treated as second-class citizens. This erroneous deduction probably comes from common knowledge that during Orthodox services there is a separate place in the sanctuary for women apart from the men. They reason from this fact that if they get involved in Judaism they will have to "lower" themselves as humans to men which they are understandably unwilling to do.

But just the oppose is true. Judaism is a religion that holds women in the highest regard. The fact that women are separated from men in the most pious Jewish sanctuaries is explained later in the chapter but it's not because they are secondary, but because of the innate power HASHEM gifted them that is essential within the female gender.

Another erroneous deduction out there is that according to the Torah HASHEM made a woman from the rib of Adam as an "equal helper." Many women only see, and can't get past, the "helper" part and therefore reject the religion in its entirety, throwing the baby out with the bath water. Instead, the focus should rightfully be on the "equal" part. The fact is that *each* gender "helps" the other, "equally."

Judaism reveres the female gender more than most other religions. There are many females, not just males, in the Torah who are Prophets. Did you know that? You probably didn't. Sarah, Rachel, Rebecca, and Leah are venerated in the Torah. Do you know about Ruth, Naomi, Esther, Hannah, and Miriam? Did you know that Deborah was a wise and courageous Judge?

Did you know that the woman is tasked with control of sex in the bedroom? You probably don't know that there are some Jewish rituals that women are exempt from because they are considered more "naturally righteous" than men. Jewish women dress "modestly" by their own definition, not a definition handed down or demanded by men. So as we go on in the explanation of Judaism women should know that this religion not only honors the "equality" of women but also expects their essential contribution to the family and the world at large. Now you know about how important women are to Judaism!

Generally speaking, there are three denominations of Judaism known as Reform, Conservative, and Orthodox. But also, there is a range of observance and ritual within each denomination, causing some congregations to be more or less pious, depending on whom you talk to. The following are very brief summaries of the denominations and the differences between them.

Those already "into" an Orthodox, Conservative, or Reform Jewish community have their own thing going on and they are always very welcoming to new people. But the Jewbie has to be somewhat willing to put in effort to pursue their Jewishness. There will be places and services that you just don't like or don't feel comfortable in for whatever reason. That's OK. Just keep trying. Don't kill your engagement of Judaism in its entirety because of one service. Eventually you'll end up someplace and someplace is better than no place. Within my own exploration I saw many, many non-religious Jews out there just like me who wanted to "get in" but didn't quite know how. The main thing to know is that you have to keep trying.

Within the Orthodox community there is a wide divergence of observance from the Modern Orthodox to the Ultra-Orthodox to Chabad and others to be sure, and also Ashkenazi (European) and Sephardic (Spanish) divisions. The traditions of each cause differing ways to observe in their services. But they are all very similar in the main.

The Modern Orthodox denomination allows for baseball caps instead of yarmulkes for head coverings outside the synagogue as well as other forms of "normal" clothing of the predominant culture. However, head coverings are still worn everywhere. The Ultra-Orthodox are always dressed the same in white shirts, black suits, and black hats. Everyone, in all Orthodox services, wear prayer shawls (extras are on hand) in the sanctuary.

All Orthodox services are conducted mostly in Hebrew. There is no Cantor, a man who sings prayers in Hebrew. Women are segregated by a half-wall so as not to affect weak minded males who are easily distracted from their prayers by the innate power of a woman's physical presence. Even the scent of a woman might arouse prurient thoughts. There is no place for Politics within Orthodox services.

The Conservative denomination also has a wide spectrum of observance. Yarmulkes are worn within the Temple but very few wear them outside. Some congregations require prayer shawls (extras are on hand), some don't. Services are conducted half in English and half in Hebrew. Male Cantors are prevalent and a centerpiece of services and all Rabbis and Cantors are male. Women are not segregated in the services. Politics can be discussed but discouraged.

The Orthodox are observant all day long so they tend to go into their services, do their business, and get out. Conservatives spend much less daily time relating to HASHEM outside the Temple so when they get to their services they tend to go on and on and on for several reasons. They believe that the longer the service the more they show they care. Also, the longer the service the more they display how "into it" they are. The Conservative denomination is the halfway point between the heavily religious Orthodox practice and the much less demanding Reform observance.

The Reform congregations "break all the rules" or should I say, "modify rules as they go along." In my opinion, they tend to believe they are smarter than every Jew that lived prior to their existence and they might very well be. I won't judge. Because of their "living Torah" point of view (a Torah whose interpretation needs to be redefined to represent current cultural lifestyles) their services tend to be very lively and include lots of musical instruments. Their services and beliefs allow for some things that are specifically not permitted in the Torah.

It's not uncommon for Reform services to be led by female Rabbis and female Cantors, both of whom are usually extremely competent at what they do. If that appeals to you, go for it. And there are usually lots of musical instruments (I've seen as many as five) and high-tech gear such as big screen monitors.

Reform services are almost totally in English. Of course there is no segregation of women because women are "equal" and men "should be" strong enough to not give in to their more prurient inclinations. Reform congregations offer marriage services to gay couples whereas the Conservative denominations generally don't do so and the Orthodox denominations definitely don't do so.

The Reform denomination is often the first stop for Jewbies and it does take them out of the Idiot Jew category on the Jewish spectrum of observance. Congratulations! The effort to learn, grow, meet nice people, and move away from the pit of secular ways is a positive step. The Reform denomination is easy and comfortable. Most men wear head coverings in the sanctuary but it's not mandatory. Politics are very often part of the sermon and are almost always from a liberal/left perspective. If you lean "Progressive" this will be a turn on. If you are Conservative politically you will be happier if you can locate a more "traditional" Reform congregation but they aren't easy to find.

You should also know that there is such a thing within Judaism known as "halachah." This is "Jewish Law." But Jewish "laws" have been argued by Jewish Sages for thousands of years. Everybody is somewhat "right" and nobody is always "right." Two Jews sitting together are known for their three opinions.

So each sect in each denomination maintains its own halachahic traditions. Halachah dictates the way holidays are observed, the ways of kosher preparations, and more. Its "the way" things are "supposed" to be done. There is one "right" way and each denomination has its own version of it.

So, you see, the spectrum of Jewishness lives in all the communities from the least observant to the most pious. And you *will* find your own sweet spot.

You don't even have to go to Friday night or Saturday morning Shabbat services to move off the Idiot Jew location on the Jewish spectrum of observance in my opinion. If you don't go to these services it's your loss. You just aren't ready yet. It's OK. Just engage in some sort of Torah study. Torah study will naturally activate your personal mitzvah (good deeds) tool. Simply taking a class at a nearby Temple *is* Torah study. You probably didn't know that. Study Torah and you make HASHEM happy!

Try taking classes offered at all the different denominations. It doesn't matter. They are free everywhere and Rabbis love to see Jewbies. Look classes up online at the Temples located near you. Almost all synagogues have them. Don't be afraid of classes offered at the more religious Orthodox or Chabad locations. The wealth of Jewish knowledge is extremely broad and stimulating. Chabad was created just for this reason, to provide places of Jewish learning.

And don't be afraid if there are only one or two other people in the class. No one is going to look down on your level of observance. The Rabbis are happy to have you there and like all good teachers they will stretch you but they won't break you. If I like a class and take it for several weeks I usually offer a donation. Usually, they never ask but it's the right thing to do. Any amount is appreciated and I usually figure $10-$15 per class paid at the time of the class or monthly.

Abraham is famous for saying, "Always learn something new every day." And he was a guy who knew a thing or two.

CHAPTER VI

The Torah of Truth

Beginning this chapter about the Torah of Truth with a conversation on sex, drugs, and rock & roll may seem sacrilege but that only proves what an Idiot Jew I used to be.

I received an athletic scholarship to Columbia University in New York for tennis in 1968. I really wasn't smart enough for this Ivy League college but their tennis team was awful and they were desperate to recruit anyone who had a record of wins. I was never a great student. All I ever wanted to do was play ball, any kind and all kinds. We made up bat and ball games on my street and I always excelled. I was almost always Captain and when we would pick players for our teams I would always take the weakest player, just for the challenge of it. I never studied in school and made only average grades. My college admission test scores were the bare minimum required for the Ivy League.

I also received a four-year athletic scholarship to attend Blair Academy, a prep school located in New Jersey at the age of 14. I was the first one to bring marijuana onto the campus. You could say I was "fashion forward." At Columbia I did the same thing and started getting interested in psychedelic drugs. I was very careful as there wasn't much scientific information on these mind-altering substances at the time and I liked competing in Tennis. It became clear to me early on that for me to get passing grades at Columbia I'd have to put some effort into my studies.

As a lazy boy and completely naïve to political history I was easy prey for radical activism that was constantly available there. Young people today are unaware that both the Korean and Vietnam wars were fought with conscripted forces. The Volunteer Army had not yet been formed. People were drafted to serve whether they liked it or not. As a pot smoker I my mantras were Peace and Love and holding a gun intending to take a human life was never going to be a reality in my universe. Anti-War activism became a natural place for me to hang out.

I figured if we activists could close down the school I could play tennis, take drugs, and wouldn't have to take classes. Stupidly I thought the Professors would give us passing grades and earn class credits anyway. After a year and a half engaging in radical protests and the takeover of buildings, Columbia issued a one-semester suspension for my destructive behavior. I'll never forget the smile on the Dean's face when he told me of the suspension because he knew that taking that much time off from college would make me eligible for conscription into the military as I would lose my student deferment. He knew he'd never see me again.

Luckily, there was only one school in the entire country, Bard College, located 50 miles north in upstate New York, that had a different semester system than other college so that I could immediately enroll and not lose my deferment. I contacted the Tennis Coach who couldn't believe his good fortune and within two weeks, in the winter of 1970, I was admitted.

There I met my future wife. We lived together for 3 years, got married by a Justice of the Peace without vows (consistent with our secular lifestyle), and were divorced 1 1/2 years later. She had done LSD with Dr. Timothy Leary, a Harvard professor (the "Dr." and the "Harvard" gave him bona fides) and he was an "expand your conscience" guru. Needless to say, during this time with her my drug use increased.

However, my wife and I, as "brilliant" as we were, intrinsically knew that the drugs were not something we could take with us into old age but we also knew that the states of consciousness we were experiencing were real to us. Certainly, we reasoned, they could be achieved, in some way, without drugs.

The states of consciousness always centered around a deep connection to nature that easily led to closeness with "something else." So, we spent the next four years traveling all over the country exploring every religion we could from the Jesus Freaks to Hinduism to Buddhism to Oaspe-ism to

Black Magic (although to the practitioner of Black Magic it's always pure "White Magic").

Finally, we ended up staying with a spiritual guru at an Ashram in Canada. Unusual for this religion, the guru was a female and she was definitely spiritually advanced. She raised the consciousness level of many young people.

Although she rarely met one-on-one with any of her disciples in the Ashram, she suddenly called me in to see her privately one crisp, cold, snowy, winter morning and we sat down opposite one another in a warm, firewood-heated room. I was a little nervous. Was I not working hard enough? Did I screw up somehow? Right off the bat she smiled and asked, "So, when are you going to leave?"

Shocked, I responded, "How did you know?"

She didn't answer.

I said, "this Ashram-Guru thing doesn't quite feel right for me. Everyone here does exactly what you tell them to do and as a result everyone is spiritually advancing at a fast rate with few mistakes. But inside I keep feeling like I don't want to be told what to do so that I won't make mistakes. It's important to me to make my own decisions and learn from whatever mistakes come down the pike (incidentally, that's the crux of competitive tennis or any competitive sport, accepting the consequences of mistakes and learning not to repeat them). I'm leaving this afternoon."

Still smiling she said, "I already knew that you were leaving and that's why I called you in this morning to say goodbye. Your decision to leave and relate to God in your own way is a wise choice, wiser than any of the people who surround me seeking their relationship to God through me or because of me. Bless you!"

Her comments brought Torah to me through her because if I hadn't left right then I never would have made it to Torah. It only took thirty-eight more years to get there!

After this time consuming and exhaustive search through various religions it seemed to me, disappointingly, that there was nothing out there that was superior to Judaism, as little of Judaism as I knew. Going back to being secular and allowing a rise in my spiritual consciousness to happen "organically" was my lazy answer. So I spent the next thirty-eight years being a Jewish Idiot. I succeeded in my professional tennis career as a Coach, player, and manager of recreational facilities.

There is terrific irony I'm building up to here.

As I began studying Judaism at the age of 63 I learned about the Lubavitcher Rebbe, Menachem Mendel Schneerson, leader of the Chabad movement, who died in 1994. He was a renowned Jewish scholar of incredible intellect. Many leaders from around the world, international influencers, and well-known personalities would come to confer with him on various topics. Even such radicals as Bob Dylan, who incidentally hung out occasionally at Bard College, went to see him for advice and inspiration. The Rebbe led the Chabad

Orthodox congregation located in Brooklyn and had many thousands of followers.

The huge irony was, as it suddenly dawned on me thirty-eight years later, that after traveling the world for four years seeking a spiritual home for myself and ultimately failing, the man I *should have seen* was only a subway car ride away from Columbia! Wow, what a complete Idiot Jew I was! How would that have changed my life if I had experienced him forty years earlier! In spite of this, I am very thankful that *eventually* I found my way back to Judaism. Now it's your turn.

This brings me to the Torah, "the Torah of Truth." Simply stated, the Torah contains righteous laws and true teachings. If you don't believe it, then read it and give me examples where the laws are not righteous. The Old Testament contains 24 books and the English translation runs about 1330 pages. The Torah is called the five books of Moses, the first 5 of the 24, and the English translation runs about 300 pages. Although the Torah was ostensibly "given" to Abraham 3500 years ago, it wasn't "written" until Moses did so along with receiving the Ten Commandments 2500 years ago on Mt. Sinai.

There are a couple of things I'd like to mention here. Firstly, there has to be something very valuable in a book that a lot of people read for 2500 years through time.

Secondly, books that last that long, especially translated into many different languages, can easily get "changed" or distorted. That didn't happen with the Torah. The Torah was written in Hebrew, the language HASHEM and Moses used to communicate, and Jewish law states that if the scribe writing the scroll makes even one mistake with a brushstroke, the entire effort must be thrown out and begun anew.

This means that every Torah written from then until now is identical in the Hebrew language. If Torah scrolls were trashed for a single errant brushstroke, it would be impossible to change even one word. You can be confident that there have been no changes made to the Torah in the last 2500 years. There are some slight changes through translation into other languages that simply can't be avoided. But if you are a purest you can learn Hebrew and read the Torah, unchanged from the original, just the way it was delivered at Mt. Sinai 2500 years ago. Although this might not amaze you, it amazes me!

What on Earth has withstood this test of time? What physical structure hasn't crumbled? Egyptian pyramids stand today but what do they tell us? What do they teach us? What morals and values do they impart to us? The Torah still stands after all this time in its perfection, purity, and beauty, chock full of intelligence, teaching morals and values; clean as the day it was delivered. If that isn't intriguing for you, I don't know what is.

"How does the Torah teach us?" you might ask in your naïveté. Here are just two little examples I've chosen of the infinite variety of lessons that can be gleaned by reading the Torah. These lessons relate to then and they relate to now.

The first has to do with the Exodus, enslaved Jews leaving Egypt for freedom and liberty. Aren't you a Jew enslaved by your attachment to secular materialism? And when you finally make the decision to leave your own personal Egypt aren't you going off into a "wilderness" with barely anything at all, not knowing where you are going, with Egyptian (secular) armies running after you, having to trust in HASHEM for everything? It worked out for the Jews then and it will work out for you now.

The second example has to do with the war between the newly freed slaves and Amalek as described in the Torah. Amalek, you will learn, is the archenemy of the Jews. When the Jews are first getting started on their trek through the desert there were stragglers, the weakest and most vulnerable, in the back of the procession. They were attacked by the nation of Amalek. Likewise, after you make a firm decision to leave your old secular life and pursue a greater enjoyment of life by increasing Jewish ritual and study, doubt, the straggler in the back of your mind, attacks and makes war with you. Amalek, doubt, assaults your decision at your most vulnerable place.

The Jews win this war in the end, you'll have to study it to find out how, but not without some pain and loss. This little story, in passing, within a chapter in the Torah, warns you about what might happen if your dedication to Him wavers and then the Torah shows you the way to overcome the challenge.

Lessons like these are nothing new and have been going on with others like you for 2500 years. If you don't study the wonderful Torah you don't get the benefits contained within it. And there are 330 pages of little stories just like this with lessons upon lessons to be gleaned in this faultless manuscript. The stories are quite basic but discovering the underlying lessons are the fun of it all!

The Christian New Testament and the Islamic Koran have also lasted through time, but not nearly as long. In the same way they probably have many valuable lessons to be learned. However, not pejoratively, Jews ask the questions: "Did HASHEM get it wrong the first time? (He needed a second "New" try?); Did HASHEM get it wrong the second time as well? (He needed a third "Koran" try?); Were 24 books, 1300 pages, not enough?"

I'm not knocking these other disciplines. I'd prefer being around Christians and Muslims than secularists because the former live by the teachings of a "good" book and the latter live by whatever feels good that day. And let's not forget, the Judeo-Christian ethic, revolving around the Ten Commandments, delivered the greatest country, the only country, of Liberty and Freedom that has ever been created, the United States of America.

So, the Torah of Truth lives on even today. You should check it out!

CHAPTER VII

Torah Study Benefits

Torah study brings benefits that change you. It doesn't necessarily bring pockets full of money and ice cream, although it might. The benefits that occur are actually much more subtle than riches and sweets.

The more you study the more you become inwardly peaceful. The more you study the more you bring really good people into your life. The more you study the more you are able to handle life's difficulties because the "right" answer to everyday situations happens quickly. It's called "righteousness" and comes about when the Secular perspective you currently use to deal with the world transmutes into a Biblical perspective. Here are some big and small illustrations.

One of the biggest things you learn from Torah study is that negative situations that happen to you are *your* fault, not someone else's. If you don't like what's going on in your life, *you* need to change it. Don't expect someone else to change it. This means that you will become naturally more self-conscious, viewing your actions in the world with greater clarity. Most secular people have little self-consciousness so they are able to lie as easily as they breathe.

If a problem presents itself, turn to *yourself* and ask, "How can I change this." Maybe you can and maybe you can't, but relying on someone else somewhere else gives away the Power you already have. Torah teaches you about this Power, how to find this Power that exists within you, and the ways in which you can exercise it. The Power is valuable so stop giving it away. Imagine that. The Torah strikes with righteous advice again!

One of the most obvious examples of giving away the Power comes through analyzing the position of Blacks in the United States. After the Reverend Dr. Martin Luther King was assassinated, and thanks to shakedown artists like Jesse Jackson and Al Sharpton, some politicians conveniently took up the task of "helping" the Black community. Their solution was to increase welfare and they gave monetary rewards for having children out of wedlock. The more children you had the more money you received. Now, where in the Torah does it say that giving monetary rewards to unwed mothers is a good thing? It doesn't. Charity as stated in the Torah is a good thing, but not given in this fashion.

The Black community, unfortunately, eagerly took the handouts and by doing so gave away the Power to politicians to solve their problems. The result is that the Black family today is totally decimated. And all they know now is to continually ask politicians for more free stuff. The only way back to decency and success is for them to reclaim their Power by working on what they can achieve *themselves*.

For 50 years I've watched "programs," meaning handouts, do nothing to advance our Black brethren. Black Lives Matter continues this vapid idea as they do what they do in order to get things from other people. The ultimate is "reparations," requesting payouts from people who never owned slaves. I don't see the Chinese seeking reparations for building the American railroad or Jews seeking reparations from Egypt for their enslavement. Agitating for the Black community Black Lives Matter, in reality, give away their Power by violently demanding increased financial benefits from others and seeking access to additional opportunities that they are unlikely to be qualified for.

The only ones getting out of the ghetto today are other shysters (who, incidentally, in their own disgusting way, *are* helping themselves) or those few who grasp the mantle of educating themselves, as Abraham advocated grasping the power, so that they can attain upwardly mobile employment opportunities through real merit.

Affirmative Action is another solution offered by vote seeking Politicians and accepted by those who give away their own personal power. Those who failed to achieve in High School are "helped" by getting admissions to college in order for them to attain a degree. Studies have shown that because they were unable to meet the standards in the first place, many end up failing and dropping out, never to attain that degree. The psychological damage to that person, failing again, does immeasurable damage. Had they relied on their own power to study and matriculate through High School they would have the skills to achieve their own admittance and success in college.

Dr. King preached "the content of your character, not the color of your skin." You build the content of your character through hard work and study no matter what the color of your skin. But it's much easier to use the color of your skin as the only qualification for free stuff. Dr. King would be called an Uncle Tom in today's "sophisticated" American culture. That's how far we've fallen morally. Dr. King, rarely referred to as a Reverend (a real Reverend as opposed to Jackson and Sharpton), was not a secular man. His Power was great.

The word Torah means "instruction." As you study Torah your perspective changes. It moves from a Secular perspective into a Biblical perspective. Everything you possess has come from HASHEM. The mate you have, your money, your stature within the community all came from HASHEM. HASHEM gave you the brains, the good looks and health, the opportunity, and the drive to gain. If you think it was all you, fine, run with that. Eventually you'll realize who to be grateful to and how fortunate you've been.

The secular person "prays" to win the lottery and spends too much of his meager income on tickets. The biblical person prays for guidance, wisdom, health, and energy. The secular person prays for someone else to provide for him while the biblical person prays for divine help in how he can provide for himself, his family, and his community.

The founding of the United States of America was a Judeo-Christian experiment that brought about Capitalism through freedom and liberty. Capitalism, for the first time in the sorry history of the planet Earth, created more wealth for more people than at any time ever. You'd think people would become more religiously inclined because of that, but they haven't. Just the opposite has transpired. Talk about killing the Golden Goose!

Unfortunately, the great prosperity provided by Capitalism fuels an increase in *secular* attitudes. People become wealthy and then shower their offspring with goodies. Their offspring then become "entitled" to everything they have without any thought as to where it came from. "Trust Fund Babies" today rarely attend religious services. Why should they? They have more exciting things to do like driving fast new cars, traveling to foreign lands, taking mind altering substances, and exploring deviant behavior. Pray for peace on Earth? You've got to be kidding.

I asked a very rich man once if he gave annually some of his income to charity (the Torah suggests 10%-20%). "Of course," he replied. "I give more than I should in tips to the wait staff at all the restaurants I eat at." I was so shocked at the arrogance of his reply that my tongue was totally tied! After all, doesn't charity mean giving without receiving? But from a Secular perspective he was giving more than the appropriate 15%-20% expected to people of a lower income level than he. That's his definition of "charity" and is not unusual from a Secular perspective.

In his mind, the fact that they treated him extra special (they jumped at the sight of him walking through the door) at the expense of serving others at the restaurant was just a side benefit that didn't involve his "charity" at all. He rationalized that it was their choice to treat him in a special way. Incidentally, he is a JINO secular Trust Fund Baby. He never worked a day in his life, lives in a big house, and buys a new car every year. His "job" is to research and seek out capital preservation investments. He considers himself a "good" person for all the "charity" he gives to the wait staff throughout the year. And he never even lights Chanukah candles.

The Torah presented to humanity the Ten Commandments. Just trying to live by the Ten Commandments is a full-time experience. It's easy not to steal candy from the candy store. It's easy to return extra change when the checkout person makes a mistake right in front of you.

But consider this. I play tennis at a city owned tennis center in a town where I used to live. Then I moved outside the city. I continued to play there unknowingly paying the same amount as if I still lived there. One of my buddies paid for me one day and told me he paid my fee and it was still at the city resident rate and I shouldn't change it, a typical secular outlook. Next time out I went to the front desk and informed them of my non-resident status. They changed it in their computer and I paid, then and thereafter, the higher non-resident fee. I didn't have to do that. But the Ten Commandments instructed me that it was the right thing to do.

It's not my money. It's HASHEM'S money. If He wants me to go broke so that I can't pay the higher fee, either I'll find a less expensive place to play or not play at all. This perfectly illustrates how your life changes when you allow a Biblical perspective to enter your life. Am I screwing myself? I don't think so. That's my Power, my choice. And I'm not playing a holier-than-thou game here in using this example. In a similar situation you can act in whatever fashion you like. I'm just showing you how a Biblical perspective changes how you deal with life.

I once started a GoFundMe campaign for a surgical operation for my dog. A friend suggested that if my appeal went directly to friends, around GoFundMe, I could save on the 15% commission they charge. I responded that Gofundme provides a unique service for which they deserve their commission. And I told him I was grateful that they didn't charge 20%! (Grateful is a Jewish thing. What's so bad about that?) Again, this is just another simple example of the Biblical perspective getting you to live less larcenously.

Do you want to know more about the Biblical perspective vs. the Secular perspective (there's more in Chapter XIV) and how it changes your life? From the Biblical perspective you soon realize that words have meaning. You choose your words carefully and you hear words differently.

An example of this is the phrase that is new in our culture and I've heard used only by those who are secular, "I wouldn't lie to you." What does that actually mean? It means, "I lie all the time" but "I wouldn't lie to *you*." Oh really? I'm special? You would never lie to *me* but you lie to others?

It's a terrible phrase. It admits a sin while creating the same sin again. Of course they will lie to you. They are liars. They admit it. A devout person would never say such a thing. Lying is not part of their universe. They live their lives conscious of always being honest and if they happen to fail, as might happen on some rare occasions because no one is perfect, it eats them up inside and they almost always correct it as best they can.

A similar phrase, "To tell you the truth," has been around a lot longer in our culture but contains the same intention. "I don't always tell the truth but right now I'm telling *you* the truth." I had a doctor say the same phrase over and over. "To tell you the truth your blood pressure is too high. To tell you the truth it might cause organ damage. To tell you the truth you need to take medication." It drove me nuts.

I got another doctor, not because I thought he was lying to me so much as it displayed a certain character flaw that he was somewhat insecure about every diagnosis and every suggestion he made. I didn't want a doctor filled with fear or doubt. My new doctor told me the same things without saying, "To tell you the truth." He gave me his best shot and if it turned out he was not quite right he'd give me his next best shot without constantly announcing doubt or fear.

These examples might seem picky but they are good illustrations of how what you say and what you hear changes when you go from the Secular perspective to the Biblical perspective. When a secular person hears from a politician that their health insurance "won't go up ten cents" they think that the cost of their health insurance won't go up. From the Biblical perspective a person hears the same thing and knows that the cost of their health insurance won't go up ten cents because it will go up many *dollars*. Who ends up hearing the truth? And, by the way, the politician didn't exactly lie, did he?

Now this is not to say that devout people never sin or are exactly precise every time they speak. It's in the trying that changes you. And you get a lot better at it with practice and the change in your perspective happens very organically.

There is a delightful Israeli TV series on Netflix entitled "Shtisel" that is about an Orthodox Jewish family whose artist son caused problems because he was unable to find a wife. Every character performed every act required within the Orthodox Jewish discipline. They said a prayer every time they ate something. They studied Torah. They observed the Sabbath perfectly. You get the idea.

Even so, as they carried out these daily obligations, they all "pushed the envelope" morally. Within this Jewish discipline they all still connived and finagled. They were human with failings. But I found it interesting that with all their devout actions of praying, studying, observing traditional meals, holidays, etc., they still were working their own way through the Ten Commandments just like I do and just like you will.

As you polish away your secular perspective, you'll realize that essentially you are trying your best to do the right thing all the time. Being more self-conscious and accepting the Power to change yourself and the world becomes a constant endeavor. Even as a tiny Jewbie you are bringing more of HASHEM into the world. Good for you!

These small examples show you how Torah Study and living the Ten Commandments will definitely change you. I can't tell you exactly how because they will change you differently than they changed me. But taking action by adding some Jewish rituals and Torah study *will* change you. It's a little scary, but not really. It's subtle and you'll like it.

What you won't expect is how this whole change thing gathers momentum. Changes in you will happen faster and faster. But that's not a bad thing. So what have you got to lose? Just do it!

Every morning when I read the Torah, I'm exercising my will to reach the divine. I'm sure you won't understand this yet but what I see is always new, never boring, and in fact quite remarkable. I'm spending time in awe. You will get to awe as well!

CHAPTER VIII
What Will Happen To You As It Happened To Me

This is my story of what occurred over a period of eight years, from the age of 63 through the age of 70. It started slowly and gained momentum. And you should start slowly and advance at your own pace. I envy those who are younger and have more time. But that's your story, not mine.

Although I know of four instances where people in their late twenties became full blown Orthodox (one becoming a Rabbi), let's face it, that's very unlikely to happen to you. So don't worry. You'll keep of your old self what you like and the parts of your old self that currently hold you back will gradually fade away on their own. What does happen by adding a bit of Jewish ritual is that that feeling that you call "spiritual" gradually and imperceptivity grows and grows and moves you to a place of greater light, safety, and intelligence. Right now it's just sitting there nagging at you.

An example of this gradual awakening for women is that

you will begin to enhance your purity and modesty instead of always trying to be sexy and alluring. Great men prefer the former to the latter and you will, first of all, save time by being ignored by the "players" and, second, be sought after by really good guys. Do you want a player or do you want a good guy?

I've often suggested to really nice young women that if they want to save time in their search for a good guy that they should tell someone they just met that they want a lot of children. And they should do it in the very first conversation. The "bad" guys will exit pronto. A good guy will probably smile and stick around. Children and family are a strong point of attraction for a good guy. What better way to start a relationship than that common goal?

And for men who start advancing spiritually you will begin to zero in on what you really want instead of "seeing the whole world as your oyster." This type of focus pinpoints where you spend your time. Believe it or not, constantly getting pleasured by a host of different women *does* get old and stale. One day you'll realize you are the oldest man in the room and you've already had it all. You've traded all that sex and pleasure for what you have now, which is nothing.

Do you really want a woman who is so sexy and alluring other men will continuously see her as prey to be devoured? Shouldn't she be sexy and alluring only to you within the privacy of your own home? Aren't purity and modesty valuable character traits? Aren't you really seeking someone who is honest and dependable, will support your morals and values, and is devoted to instilling them into your children? You think you'll find that woman in a bar or restaurant? I guess it could happen, but probably not.

That "spiritual" feeling you readily admit to, you like that feeling. Surrounded by that feeling there is a certain sense of calm that protects you from the worries of the secular world. Politics? Whatever. Money worries? Somehow it works out. Marital conflicts? The disappointments don't drag you down so much and acceptance of them makes you see other things to be grateful for.

The main driver of all this will be your increasing attention to knowing more about your religion and doing more of the rituals attached to your religion. Go slowly, within your comfort zone. The things you think will turn you off about religious practice will really not be so bad. It's fine to move forward into something and then move back a few steps. It's all a process and you will be progressing regardless.

I went from attending Shabbat services once per month on Friday nights to attending every week, because it felt good and I wanted to. What's the big deal? It's just one hour out of the week. I didn't go to Saturday services. Maybe you'll choose Saturday over Friday or even do both. Just getting into it is the mission.

After a while I started lighting Shabbat candles. Now when I glance at the candles and see them burning it reminds me that it's quite a pleasant ritual. Candle lighting is traditionally reserved for females who, when doing so, connect with all Jewish females around the world. In my case as a single man, if there are no females in the house then males are permitted to do it.

Lighting Shabbat candles includes saying a prayer. It's a short prayer, easy to memorize even for an Idiot Jew. The Hebrew translation into English is always provided wherever you go on an Internet search to look for it. When you take one minute out of your mundane life to light Shabbat candles and say the short prayer it changes you. And every time you spy the burning candles they lift you.

Early on I decided I should buy a Siddur, the Jewish book of prayers for all occasions, and there are surprisingly lots of occasions. It contains 600 pages on one side in Hebrew and 600 pages on the other in English. It's a good thing to have around even if it just sits there on a table blowing holy vibes throughout your house.

At this point I was inspired to spend one hour every morning with my Jewish learning, simply reading about Judaism. Rabbis recommended books for me. It really set me up for the entire day. The days I missed seemed somewhat lacking. The days I forced myself to engage ended up being wonderful days. A habit was forming and I was obviously advancing in my knowledge of the world and the interactions I was having within it.

Previously I excelled at Tennis, was better than average at Golf and West Coast Swing dancing. But those disciplines only rewarded *me*. Now I was discovering that because of my studies, not only was my life more pleasant, but also I was having a positive effect on other people. My presence in the world had so much more meaning for me and also the people I was interacting with.

Pursuing my spiritual feeling by adding a bit of "religious ritual" was changing me into someone who was affecting other people, making *them* better. It's said that HASHEM gave the Torah so that he could become more present in the physical world. Well, in my own little way, wasn't this bringing a little bit of Him into the world?

I was intrigued by the fact that Moses spoke to HASHEM in the Hebrew language so I decided I'd try to master that huge task. Unfortunately it beat me, but well worth the effort as it increased my admiration for those who can read and understand the history and prayers of our religion in the purest form, just the way it was transmitted at Mt. Sinai 2500 years ago.

I tried hard though. I took a beginner class in Hebrew and then started getting private Hebrew lessons. When HASHEM was handing out athletic ability I was somewhere near the front of the line. When he was handing out language abilities I was in the restroom. It took me four years to complete a two-year requirement to pass high school Spanish, a language with letters I knew and pronunciations I could figure out.

In learning Hebrew I was looking at not only new alphabet shapes of letters but also new pronunciations including vowel renderings! Most advanced readings of Hebrew don't even include the vowel renderings! You just have to know the words. It was all too much for me so I quit. Occasionally I still dabble in it a little bit. But it was a challenge beyond my intellectual capacity at my advanced age No matter. Sometimes you gain knowledge, sometimes you don't. There is plenty more to learn in Judaism.

In spite of all this I did learn how to read Hebrew phonetically very, very, very slowly. But I didn't understand a word of what I was reading, no vocabulary whatsoever. Later I discovered that most people who attend Reform and Conservative services and who read fluently from the Torah when called to the Bima (a raised stage where the Torah is read in the sanctuary) also don't understand a word of what they are reading. (I'm sure you didn't know that) But it's all "OK." In Judaism, whatever place you sit on the ritual spectrum is just fine with HASHEM. That's the beauty of the religion, having your own relationship with HASHEM.

Within my attempt at learning Hebrew I did manage to read through my entire Siddur of 1200 pages, 600 in English and 600 in Hebrew. I was midway through doing it again when I realized that learning the meaning of the Hebrew words was way above my pay grade. So because of this and my slow reading speed I stopped putting time into it. The religion is so large, and the remainder of my lifespan becoming more and more limited, that I decided to put my "study" energy elsewhere. You too will have gains and losses when you start studying. It's normal. Find your niche and run with it.

After attending "outreach" services in the basement classroom of the Orthodox Temple in Florida, I found myself missing that experience when I traveled to New York for the summer months. Nearby where I lived there was a Friday night Shabbat service. It was a "traditional" Reform presentation. The Rabbi rented space on Friday nights in a delightful, small, Christian Chapel. I liked the service but it was very sparsely attended. Eventually the Rabbi was hired to serve at a larger congregation much further away from where I was living, too far away for me to attend.

When that service vanished, I tried other Friday night services at all different denominations. Most of them didn't seem to give me the "juice" I was seeking but the experience of other services was elucidating. You will probably go through the same thing. Eventually you will find a congregation, or at least a Rabbi, that suits you.

But the result of this was that now I had two Rabbis that I had developed relationships with. One was Reform in New York and the other was Orthodox in Florida. Both were eager to share whatever resources were available to them. All I had to do was ask. They recommended books, lawyers, doctors, and whatever I was in need of. For me, this was a good thing and added to my life.

I also attended classes at different denominations. The ones held at Orthodox or Chabad locations I found to be the best for me. You will also gravitate to the ones that stimulate you the most, regardless of denomination. I've been attending a Chabad zoom class for several months now. There are only 2-6 people in the class but it really doesn't matter how many attend. It's very enlightening. And so now I have *three* Rabbis who I have relationships with! So you see how it all grows, organically, by expanding your world with people, both Rabbis and other seeking students, who are healthy and safe to be around.

Back in Florida at the outreach Shabbat services there was what they called a "Parsha Minute" in which the Rabbi would discuss something within the weekly Parsha. One chapter in the Torah is read in the synagogue every Saturday morning and that's what a Parsha is. Each Parsha seems to have unlimited lessons contained within it. The Parsha Minute at this Friday night service was sometimes actually a minute but never lasted more than five minutes. But this brief encounter with the weekly Torah portion seduced me into looking further into it.

It seemed reasonable to me that I should start reading the entire weekly Parsha on my own prior to the Shabbat service. After all, it only takes about a half hour each week to do so. Big deal. Jews had been doing this for 2500 years. Why shouldn't I? Why shouldn't you? There had to be some wisdom in there somewhere for it to be going on continuously for that many years. When you first start reading these weekly chapters, you'll see nothing there, no wisdom, nothing but a story and sometimes a disjointed story. That's where "Torah Study" comes in. Sometimes the deeper meanings are brought out at Friday or Saturday services and sometimes at a class you might take. The levels of interpretation and wisdom then come through.

Now, much is lost in translation from Hebrew to English so I didn't understand much of what I was reading even though I was reading the Parshas in English, but nevertheless it instigated discussions that brought light into what was actually there. And all this "stuff" seemed to be "expanding my consciousness," exactly what my mission was before running all over the planet 40 years earlier looking for spiritual experiences without drugs!

Eventually I really got hooked on the history of the Jews and began reading contemporary books on Jewish history. I was curious about how they built their homes, their occupations, what they ate, how they found water, where they pooped. But here's the takeaway from all my reading: Jews get terribly slaughtered about every one hundred years. Those that survive always replenish their numbers and become great scholars and merchants. Then they get slaughtered again. It seems cruel, and it is, but I've found no answer for it.

The really amazing part is that throughout history wherever Jews are welcomed by the existing culture, that culture thrives. The culture that wipes them out or expels them goes right into decline. You'd think that leaders of other cultures around the world would know their history, but apparently they don't and mostly likely are too stupid to be aware of this pattern in world history.

It then occurred to me that there was a Koran, a New Testament, and an Old Testament. All of these books contain great wisdom. Did the New Testament improve on the Old? Did the Koran improve on the New Testament? Did HASHEM get it wrong the first time and needed a clarifying, "new" testament? And then he got it not quite right the second time and needed the Koran? I don't know but I figured I should at least start from the beginning of it all and read the Old Testament. And so should you. It will keep you occupied for a lifetime and you won't need a second or third treatise.

So, what exactly is stopping you? You can't take an hour, stop the world, and improve yourself? I know exactly what's stopping you, the final obstacle that's holding you back. You are afraid that all your friends will accuse you of "going religious." They are all, just like you used to be, indifferent to religious practice. It's a very cold position to take.

Understand that your friends are expressing their own apathy to grow closer to their essence. If they are non-Jews, it will be impossible for them to know exactly what the Jew spark is within you. If they are Jewish then you very well could be the inspiration that takes them out of their own material slavery as they see your enthusiasm for Judaism increase. This enthusiasm is a warm position to take. If they truly are a friend to you, wouldn't they want you to grow and have less indecision in your life?

Being "religious" on the inside doesn't change you on the outside. It might modify how you relate to the outside world but you are still the same person. You will still enjoy restaurants, go to the gym, get your hair done, and do what you usually do. So let them call you whatever they want. They have the freedom to make their choices and you have the freedom to make yours. But as your life improves you'll know that this new "discipline" of yours is a good thing for you and also everyone around you.

HASHEM wants you to bring more of Him into the physical world. So get started now!

CHAPTER IX
HASHEM: THE WORLD'S GREATEST COMEDIAN

People ascribe many great qualities to HASHEM. He's the All Powerful. He Judges everyone. He's Wrathful, the great Destroyer. He's kind, the Ultimate Forgiver. He creates Miracles of every kind. But did you ever consider that He's also the funniest, the One with the greatest sense of humor, by far? Consider all His plays on words.

Ronald Reagan brought down the USSR without firing a shot. He used a Ray-Gun.

Two Bushes did not even equal a tree.

Then there was the Obama Nation, the abomination, eight years of nothing but White House drug parties and the only legislation passed was a poorly designed, partisan, health care system that served only a few people at the expense of a lot of people.

Hillary was quite the hilarity.

Was it only me who found it interesting that Donald

Trump trumped every smear and attack that was thrown at him from before he took office and for the four years of his Administration?

And of course, Dog spelled backwards is God. How funny is that? We all know how much we unconditionally love our dogs! There is a sublime message in there.

Speaking of backwards, the name Moses in Hebrew is Moshe. Moshe spelled backwards in Hebrew is HASHEM.

Just look at what a smile is. Don't we all smile for a picture? The reason is we look our best that way. Even a dog's smile is a beautiful thing. HASHEM didn't need to make smiles as a part of this whole Creation thing. But He did.

I'm sure there's much, much more but you get the gist of it. In addition to HASHEM'S seriousness, demands, and piety, we should also always be looking for the humor in His Creation.

I see it all the time and laugh!

CHAPTER X

Idiot Rabbis

In many ways Idiot Rabbis are worse than Idiot Jews. Rabbis should know better.

Idiot Jews only hurt themselves. Idiot Rabbis hurt their congregants.

A Rabbi becomes an Idiot Rabbi when he brings politics into his sermons or his lessons. A Rabbi is a Rabbi because of his theological training. People come to the synagogue for theology. And there is plenty of theology to transfer to the congregation without getting political.

There are many in the congregation, myself included, that studied Political Science. I know more in this realm than most Rabbis. Every time I've heard a Rabbi go political it has always been at an incredibly unsophisticated level. So my respect for that particular Rabbi immediately drops. This is not a good thing.

If you are a professional hockey player don't try to play professional football. It doesn't work. Both are contact tough sports. But you'll get crushed no matter how big and tough you think you are because they don't translate seamlessly. Rabbis similarly get crushed when they dabble in politics. Idiots.

It never occurs to an Idiot Rabbi that there are many in the congregation who don't share their political viewpoints. These are the ones who are squirming in their seats wondering how to gracefully get up and leave. It might be half the congregation, or more, or less. Whatever the amount you've totally turned them away from you as a deliverer of uplifting thought and you probably have not changed their mind anyway. If it continues into other weekly sermons, they will get up and leave permanently and sometimes not so gracefully.

So, stick to what you know. Stick to what you were trained in. Your training makes you the smartest man in the room by keeping your sermons within your theological discipline. People come to Temple to hear what the Torah teaches, not what's in the New York Times. Give the people what they can't get elsewhere. Don't be an Idiot Rabbi!

And by the way, according to the law pertaining to non-profit religious institutions, the use of the pulpit to sway a congregation politically is illegal and jeopardizes your non-profit status.

Now, who am I to tell a Rabbi that he is an idiot? I'm the one writing a book about Judaism and have no theological training whatsoever. Aren't I the idiot delving into realms where I have no theological training? Yes, I am. But I've already admitted to being an Idiot Jew, I'm still entitled to my opinion, and I'm giving no theological lessons. I'm just sharing personal, Jewbie, JINO experiences of Judaism so that others can seamlessly enter into the family.

I'm attempting to point out in this book why it enhances a non-religious Jew's life to return to Judaism by adding some Jewish ritual in whatever fashion they see fit. I'm a small voice in the war against assimilation. If I succeed in bringing just one Jew back into the fold then all this time, expense, and effort will have been worth it.

CHAPTER XI

Time

Well, after the preceding, two, light and fluffy chapters, this one is going to be the hardest to understand and it's the hardest chapter for me to write, mostly because my own comprehension barely scratches the surface of the concept. But it's an important piece for the Jewbie as it will give you a jumpstart on what Judaism ultimately is. So here goes!

Man constantly conquers things in space. Man is really good at building tall buildings, flying, and lifting heavy objects. But Man is totally conquered by Time. Man can't move backward in Time nor is he able to move forward in Time, even an instant. Man loses to Time no matter how hard he tries. Man lives and dies within Time without any control whatsoever. HASHEM exists in Time, not in space. Untouchable, one aspect of HASHEM is Time. That's why He can't be seen or touched, although He has been heard.

Judaism does not see HASHEM in space, as a thing or a person, or even in Nature. Judaism sees HASHEM in Time and as Time. Judaism goes beyond monotheism even though that was as unique and earth shattering as anything that came prior to it. Once you understand this about Time and Judaism you will understand why Jews have no sacred "things" or "places" or "images" or "idols" to worship.

You might say that the Torah is a sacred "thing," and it is revered, but the Torah is not a thing of worship in itself. It's the compilation of events in Time that create a culture of learning, morals, and values. It allows us to "hear" HASHEM so that we can opine, fight, and argue about what He said in order to refine our culture, move us away from our animal nature towards the divine. Who in the world has done that more than Jews? Don't you want to claim your spot on the team?

Jews worship HASHEM in festivals, celebrations of events in Time. We experience HASHEM on the Sabbath *day*, the "time" first noted in the Bible as "Holy." We celebrate the *time* of the new moon but not the moon. All of our festivals are events that occurred at specific times such as Chanukah, Yom Kippur, Rosh Hashanah, Sukkot, Shavuot, Passover, Purim, and more. We do not worship people, places, or forms that are animate or inanimate. Events in Time describe who Jews are.

We are specifically commanded not to create idols to worship because HASHEM is so enormous that He can't be confined in one space. HASHEM is not physical, but rather spiritual. HASHEM is to be located in Time. Time belongs to HASHEM. HASHEM has infinite aspects but a major one is Time.

When you have a spiritual moment, say in the birth of a child, it's a "moment" in Time. It's you connecting with HASHEM at that moment in a very special, intense way. Even non-religious people experience it. It's not a moment of prayer, or praise, or inspiration. It's a moment of amazement so great you are hardly able to capture which sense you are responding to. The birth of the child is not HASHEM. HASHEM is the moment the child is brought into the world. It's a "thing," an event in Time.

So if there is no physical manifestation of HASHEM in space it creates a very unique situation of worship that *each individual must create.* "You shall love the Lord your God with all your heart and all your soul." The Rabbis try to enable you to grow this love with Jewish rituals because those rituals are the food of love for HASHEM. Adding some Jewish rituals to your life will feed you spiritually. But ultimately, each Jew develops his own relationship with HASHEM to the best of their ability/capacity. Only you can measure it. Isn't that cool?

You can be Jewish right now just by the quality of your love and connection to HASHEM. It is even possible for you to gain great piety in a New York instant (although probably unlikely) just by the depth of your own connection, developed by you, to HASHEM. Obviously there's more to it than that, actually maybe not, but you get my drift.

It has been said throughout all generations by all peoples,

"Time is more precious than gold." That's the great comedian HASHEM "hiding" His whereabouts with a cute expression right there in front of us!

This concept is hard to grasp and there are many very observant Jews who know nothing of it. In spite of that each Jew is developing his own unique relationship with HASHEM. And you can too. The Rabbis teach the "fear of God" in order to put HASHEM around you every moment of the day, like wearing a yarmulke on your head.

But "where" is HASHEM? Is He above you or below you? Is He to the right or left of you? Is He in front of you or in back of you? Is He with you now or later? How can he be here with you and also over there with that other person? You figure it out. That's what Jews, as opposed to other religions, do. Each individual figures it out.

Other religions tell you what and how to perceive God. Jews figure it out individually within their own Torah study. And that's what's so special about the Jewish religion and so far out into the "future" that Judaism exists. Because HASHEM is, and is the master of, Time He can do all these things (here, there, everywhere) simultaneously quite easily.

Here's the bottom line: Judaism not only allows you to create your own relationship with HASHEM but also demands that you absolutely make it personal. HASHEM is not someone else's idea that you are to conform to. It's your idea created from your own inspiration enhanced by Jewish ritual and study. For thousands of years this has been going on within the religion of Judaism. Isn't it now time for you to add your own special spice to this amazing spiritual stew? We're all waiting for your contribution!

CHAPTER XII
Fun Facts About Miracles

Miracles, miracles, miracles happened in great bunches in the history of Judaism. Are we supposed to believe them all? Well, it was a different time back 2,500 years ago. It's barely been 100 years since electricity, radio waves, nuclear physics, and hydraulics have changed the human condition. So why is it so hard to believe that miracles and prophets, none of which exist today, actually happened back then? But so what? Believe them or don't believe them. The narrations still contain life lessons, teach morals, and display values that enhance the lives of human beings everywhere.

It's perfectly reasonable to me that HASHEM finally said, "no more of this otherworldly stuff, they'll just have to come to me of their own volition without any more of this 'see it with your own eyes' assistance." Regardless, all these miracles yield wonderful stories with lessons to be learned, whether you take them literally or figuratively.

Beginning with the ten plagues many people find it hard

to believe that they actually occurred, that the Jews wandered in the desert for 40 years, and that a single one-day vial of oil would stay lit for eight days. I guess you had to be there. A Jew returning to HASHEM can believe the miracles or not. It doesn't matter. If it were one, two, or five miracles it would be easy to say it never happened. But there are so many miracles it's hard to say *none* of them ever happened.

I find it hard to believe that it's *all* made up. There doesn't seem to be much historical evidence that these things *didn't* happen. Also, if you believe it didn't happen then "there is no reason to study it" and therefore gain no wisdom into what Jews for thousands of years have gleaned.

Most secular Jews today believe they are smarter than all the humans that ever lived, Jews and non-Jews alike, prior to them. After all, we fly, we drive, and we live in homes 24 stories above the earth. How amazing are we?

The hubris of this thought process limits growth. If you really feel "spiritual" in a Jewish way, then you probably believe all the miracles. Nowhere does it say you should believe all the *miracles* "with all your heart and all your soul" but it's a foundation of Judaism that you believe in the *Creator* "with all your heart and all your soul." It just makes it easier to grow when you have some level of acceptance of the miracles that ostensibly occurred at that time. And when you invest in their study it embellishes your life. The following are many of the *big* miracles, leaving the smaller ones aside.

First, Moses brought ten plagues down on the Pharaoh

and all of Egypt. Can you imagine that it would take ten devastating plagues to get the Pharaoh to release the Hebrews? Two or three disasters of overwhelming damage should have done the trick, but ten?! The Pharaoh was obstinate to the max (lessons to be learned there). And most people imagine that the ten plagues took place over just a few weeks. It didn't. The plaques went on for over a year. Moses probably wasn't a very popular guy around Egypt at the time.

The ten plagues of the Exodus showed unequivocally that HASHEM is the only one who can control Nature. So take that climate change enthusiasts! Oh, but you don't believe that the ten plagues ever occurred so therefore there is no proof that HASHEM controls Nature. OK, knock yourself out. Nobody really cares about your perfect logic except other secularists and atheists. It takes incredible arrogance, chutzpah, and hubris to believe that man can actually affect or modify the climate of something the immense size of the Earth.

My awe of HASHEM tells me that it's quite impossible for humans to control the weather and/or the temperature of the Earth. It's like saying that someday we will be able to control Time, being able to move forward and backward in time. It just can't happen and it just won't ever happen. An ability to move back in Time and change an event also changes what occurs in the present and the ability to move forward in Time to change an event also changes what occurs in the present. Is the understanding of both of these issues, Climate and Time, a fact or a belief?

Others will come up with the fantastical idea that we MUST control the climate or "we're all going die!" They come up with computer models based on questionable data that proves "scientifically" this thesis. That's their "fact" and their reality, but it's not mine because I reach for the divine and I don't believe that we are all going to die. HASHEM is far too brilliant and Nature is far too resilient.

Throughout history there have been religious fanatics who have stood on street corners with signs saying, "The End Is Here." But their predictions of major calamities never ever happen. Instead of "religious fanatics," today we call them "environmentalists."

With no awe of HASHEM and no Faith in the climatic history of the Earth, secularists rely on their own little minds to create chaos in the world. It's an anti-mitzvah. It feeds their animal nature in the same way movies feed their animal nature. What I see is a remarkable Creation in perfect harmony. What I don't see is secularists seeking their divine nature. And if there are Jews walking the planet who don't seek their divine nature, JINOS, why should non-Jews seek it? That's why Idiot Jews need to come aboard. When they do come aboard, perhaps other Jews and non-Jews will follow. But even if non-Jews don't follow, at least it raises the Idiot Jew away from his animal nature towards the divine.

You don't have to believe that the flood of Noah's Ark

ever occurred either and other instances of HASHEM intervening in Nature. Believing whether the actual events happened is not really all that important because there are lessons to be learned in the tales regardless. Learn it, believe it, or not. It's your choice. But even Einstein (a Jew) realized that the more he studied Nature the more he believed it was created by a higher source. But go ahead believe that it all came about from nothing. Knock yourself out!

Speaking of nothing, the science of the Big Bang theory sent atheists and agnostics scampering into a tizzy. If there was a Big Bang, there must have been a Big Banger. Oh, well, another one bites the dust!

How many people left Egypt in the Exodus…a few thousand, a hundred thousand? The Torah records over three million. The census in the Torah lists 600,000 able bodied men plus their wives plus their children plus others who were male elders or the infirm. Now consider that there were 400,000 people that attended the hot mess that was the Woodstock Music Festival in 1969. Now imagine 7 times that many people! And there were livestock and tents and matzos too!

Uber didn't exist. They walked. They walked into a DESERT! But I guess as daunting a task as this wasn't so hard to accept after living through ten amazing plagues over the course of more than a year. Having faith in HASHEM was probably easy. Yeah, right!

Just as an aside, not all the Hebrew slaves chose to leave Egypt. "What? Walk into the dessert with nothing? I'd rather stay here and be a slave."

And also there were some Egyptians who were not Hebrew slaves that joined the Exodus. They probably figured Moses had some kind of juice (Jewce) that was probably better to follow than staying home with the uncompromising Pharaoh.

Amazingly, after all the plagues the Pharaoh *still* chased after Moses and the former slaves in order to exterminate them all. That's when HASHEM parted the Sea of Reeds allowing Moses and the Hebrews to cross safely. Miracles, miracles, miracles. But more than that, the timing was impeccable as the Pharaoh and his remarkably huge and heavily outfitted army was totally and completely destroyed down to the very last man when the waters came crashing down on them.

Those in the Exodus were astounded by this miracle but then yet *another* miracle occurred. The 3 million Hebrews sat down on the bank of the river and witnessed the devastation of the Pharaoh and every single one of his armed force and then sang a "song of thanksgiving," a sacred song noted in the Torah. The musicians played and the Hebrews sang the words, all at the same time, in unison. Now, this song wasn't a Lennon and McCartney tune written down, copied at Office Depot, and delivered to each person by Amazon. And yet they all "instantly" knew the melody, the lyrics, and the phrasing. How did that happen? Must have been a miracle.

Giving thanks is who Jews are. I like that. They are defined by gratitude in the definition of their name. Yehuda in Hebrew means "He who is praised." It's a word that expresses appreciation. The name Judah, Jew, is a word coming from Yehuda that means thanks or gratefulness. So when we call ourselves Jews we are saying we are the people who are thankful for everything. How wonderful is that? Don't you love, now, calling yourself a "Jew?"

Believe it or not, these miracles were just beginning. More than 3 million people walked straight into the desert with no destination and barely any food and no water. A "cloud of glory" surrounded them during the day and a "pillar of fire" at night. What? Huh? The Idiot Jew probably never heard about these two miracles. I didn't.

The clouds provided protection from the heat, kept their clothing clean, gave guidance to their march, and kept predators from seeing whom they might attack. The cloud and fire stayed with the Hebrews for 40 years. Now that's a long-running miracle!

The Hebrews did not wander constantly. You probably thought they got up and walked every day. Not so. Sometimes they would stay in one place for quite some time and sometimes they would travel just a short distance or quite a distance.

They ate "manna from heaven." This was a substance that was found on the ground every morning. People would gather up only what they would eat daily and no more. On Friday morning a double portion was collected because the manna would not fall on Shabbat. So, six days per week for 40 years the manna fell. Manna from heaven was just your "average" run-of-the-mill miracle.

Need water? Moses struck a rock with his rod and water flowed. Water coming from a rock? Can't be. What's the lesson in that miracle? Take a class and find out!

And get this. The Torah teaches that there was a time when the people complained that they were tired of manna and missed the "real" food they left behind in Egypt. So, quail fell from the sky and they ate until they were satisfied. Well, not quite satisfied because they all died from their gluttony.

Further along comes the story of the golden calf that I find quite amazing. After living through all these astounding miracles over many days 3,000 Hebrews made a golden calf to worship. Like, what, HASHEM didn't do enough for you? You need something *other* than HASHEM to worship? This is what amazes me. Some Idiot Jews just don't have the desire or capacity to learn! (But you do, otherwise you wouldn't be reading this book!)

In a slight defense of these 3,000 Idiot Jews, Moses had gone up Mt. Sinai for 40 days and they had no idea when he would return or even if he would return. Moses was the point man for all these miracles and without him these particular

Hebrews felt the need for an object of worship. But you'd think with all the miracles they'd witnessed that creating an idol would be sacrilege. Then again, Moses was up the mountain receiving the Ten Commandments so the Idiot 3,000 hadn't yet seen "Thou shall have no other Gods before me," and "Thou shall not make or worship idols."

In the end Moses came down off the mountain, got ticked off, smashed the original tablets, and the ugly 3,000 perished. It was a small minority of the congregation but still it's hard to imagine that after having actually lived through all the miracles some people would still not understand the relationship between Man and HASHEM.

So it's not surprising that today's Idiot Jew also disregards HASHEM (even though they "feel" Him spiritually) and create their own idols of fame, fortune, beauty, youth, and more. Cold apathy for HASHEM is really easy. Warm enthusiasm for HASHEM takes a little work. And so, it should be.

Esau sold his birthright to Jacob for a bowl of stew. Idiot Jews sold their birthright for a bowl of secularism.

And perhaps the biggest miracle of them all was birthing the Ten Commandments. How did they get here? Did Moses really bring them down from the mountain? You can tie yourself up in a knot trying to believe whether it happened or not. But the reality is, the Ten Commandments are here. And that's the important part.

I think you get the point about miracles. The Jews never would have made it out of Egypt or through the desert without them. And in each Torah recorded miracle there are lessons to be learned whether you believe in the reality of the miracle or not. You say you're not interested in the depth and breadth of these lessons? Fine, remain secular, and be an Idiot Jew.

Personally, I find it easy to believe the miracles. Wise men throughout the ages have also believed in the miracles. You don't want to believe in them, OK. Perhaps you are smarter than all those who lived before you. But the sages, the most intelligent of our people, have spent countless years deconstructing the Torah in order to give the morals and values contained therein to little people just like us. Those morals and values create a better world for everyone, Jews and non-Jews alike.

It's not necessary to believe in the miracles to gain the knowledge of the rich traditions of Judaism. But it all makes a bit more sense though and easier to understand the lessons inherent in them if you do.

I can't see how any Idiot Jew wouldn't be extremely impressed by Jewish history, real or imagined. When you seek and know more of the whole story you have to say to yourself, "Hey, I didn't know any of this, and now that I do I want to claim my birthright in this group. I want to live by the standards set up by this group as best as I'm able. Who else on planet Earth has expressed such divine knowledge?"

You claim your Jewish birthright just by Torah study. And

Torah study just means reading a little, attending an interesting class, and lighting a candle. So, do it!

CHAPTER XIII

Trapped Inside Secular Culture

The Idiot Jew lives within the exile of spiritual darkness of his own making. So he doesn't have to overcome a stubborn Pharaoh to get permission to walk out of Egypt. He can simply make the decision and go. It's worse than that though because he has to overcome his own stubborn stasis, his own stubborn inertia, that is constantly reinforced by outside forces that tell him there is no God and material pleasures are the end all and be all.

But the innate essence of the Idiot Jew instinctually tells him otherwise. Is that the "wee, small voice of God" that we always hear about but never quite grasp? Perhaps it's the voice of HASHEM crying out, "Hey, Idiot Jew, I'm right here. Let's go out and play!"

The problem for the Idiot Jew today is that they exist within a powerful secular environment. Many Rabbis call it "the pit." The pit contains the whole of the world's culture, everything from the "good" to the most deviant. So if you meet a charming person in a restaurant they could be a charming person or a serial rapist. You live in the pit so it could easily be either one. I guess that's the "thrill" of the pit if you want to call that thrilling. The reality is that most of the time you are defending against bad people. It makes you suspicious of everyone and everything most of the time. It colors you and not in a good way.

The Idiot Jew would never think of trying to meet someone in a Temple because those people aren't cool or trendy enough. The un-cool and un-trendy are only good, reliable and trustworthy, devoted, and try hard. What terrible qualities (sarcasm)! When you hang out with religious people you take yourself somewhat out of the pit. You may still have one foot in the pit and one foot out, but at least doing some activities with others within a spiritual setting you are not *completely* in the pit.

(Disclaimer here: I'm not saying that there aren't any religious charlatans out there. There are. I'm just saying that within the Jewish communities, all denominations considered, there is much, much less of it.)

In today's secular culture people lie, steal, and cheat as easily as they breathe. They smile, joke, live high lives but know nothing of the Ten Commandments. When the secular and the religious meet, it's like they are talking two different languages. Secular people know that it's wrong to commit adultery but when tempted "wrong" isn't an issue. Pleasure is the main goal regardless of right or wrong.

Everyone knows that lying is bad but when you tell your child to tell a phone caller that you are not home when you obviously are, you are telling that child that small lies, "white lies," are not so "bad" after all. Yet when asked, that same person would say that they teach their children to be honest at all times.

There is also this thing called "intention." In the secular world "intentions" are the get-out-of-jail-free card, literally. Violent protesters are arrested but not prosecuted because their "intentions" are considered by other secularists "good." They were protesting police brutality, racism, or any other such thing so burning down buildings, destroying the property of others, and creating mayhem is forgiven.

Secular people will take out a loan with every intention to pay it off so when they don't pay it off they are still "good" people. They just had a slight lack of finances problem.

When this happens in a religious community the person is not considered "good" no matter what their intention and they are treated at arm's length until they resolve their debt problem. Additionally, when you don't repay a debt the punishment you deserve is between you and your Creator and HASHEM will eventually do the judging of both the secular and religious regardless of your orientation.

All intentions become real only when actions make them

real. If there is no action on the intention then the intention becomes, in reality, a lie. Somehow, in the secular world today where inactions are many times ignored, a lie then becomes "good." In the religious world intentions translate into "obligations" and in the Jewish world life is filled with obligations. The more you fulfill obligations the easier it gets because you become more practiced at it. Within Jewish communities an intention, even the smallest one, is almost always carried out. I like that about Judaism.

How did intentions gain such enormous power? It used to be that if you had every intention to plant the crop but you failed to take the action, you would have no food. The secular world has changed all that. Pretty cool, huh?

Now you can fail to produce and still succeed. Excuses and rationalizations rule the day. "Have a heart." "Give them a break." You can cheat on a test and still get a college degree. You never had any intention to cheat when you entered college but in order to get the degree you "had to" cheat on the test because instead of studying properly you had other things to do. Excuses and rationalizations defeat intentions every time.

I had an experience as a young man in my twenties that was so simple yet profound. It is still so vivid that I remember it distinctly 50 years later. I was eating breakfast in a small coffee shop and when I finished the waitress (that's what we called female servers back in the olden days before the secular world destroyed the essence of both genders) gave me a check. On the back of the check she had written, "If everyone had a joyous attitude, oh what a wonderful world this would be!" I understand that simple statement even better every year HASHEM keeps me alive.

The secular world has brought us to the point where you don't have to do *anything* and you are still prized as a human being. Think Kim Kardashian. Think no-scoring sports "contests" and participation "trophies." The religious world doesn't work that way. If you have an intention then you perform the appropriate action to fulfill the intention. Fulfilling those intentions is what makes you a "good" person according to the religious perspective. If everyone fulfilled intentions, oh what a wonderful world this would be!

And what's even worse, the opposite is true. Secular people believe that if you had no intention of having a baby, then removing the fetus after conceiving it "by accident" is perfectly OK. It seems obvious that the religious believe that if you had no intention of having a baby then perhaps you shouldn't be engaging in sexual intercourse. That's the same intention with two different outcomes from two different perspectives. The former perspective permanently denies life to another human being for convenience's sake while the latter perspective never even faces the situation.

And if you do engage in sexual intercourse with no intention of conceiving a baby and you are blessed with an "accident," from the religious perspective you are then obligated to do the right thing and raise that child in a loving two-parent household. And if you are incapable of providing that, there are plenty of loving two-parent households waiting to adopt that infant. That's the right, superior thing to do because it's the best thing for the baby. If everyone did the right thing, oh what a wonderful world this would be!

Now, honestly, which culture would you rather hang out in? Do you want to surround yourself with people who lie, steal, and cheat as easily as they breathe or with people who are doing their best not to lie, steal, or cheat? Do you want to be around people who have good intentions with no follow through or around people who do what they say they will do?

The Ten Commandments are right there. Just do your best to live by them.

If you mention the Ten Commandments to a secular person their eyes glaze over. They know of them, can name a few, but they have no connection to them whatsoever. And they believe that just because you live by the Ten Commandments doesn't mean that they have to. And that is true. But that also means that you have the free choice to remove yourself from their world or deal with their world as little as possible. And that's what happens when you take baby steps to become more religious, adding just a few Jewish rituals into your lifestyle. The bad fade away and the good become more available to you. Your defense shield needn't be so rigid. If everyone lived by the Ten Commandments, oh what a wonderful world this would be!

Did it ever occur to you that for 2500 years the smartest people of your Jewish heritage, indeed the smartest people in the world, have read the Torah that contains the Ten Commandments many times over? And yet you haven't read it even once! You surround yourself with people who haven't read it either. Is that wise? If smart people have been reading it throughout millennia, don't you think there might be something in the Torah that could enhance your life even a little?

Secular culture today is in a downward spiral and you are in the middle of it. Movies, music, art, sports, everything has become political with little redeeming social value. America was founded upon a Judeo-Christian ethic based on the Ten Commandments but secularism is now winning the day. Prayer is out of the schools, the Ten Commandments are out of the Courthouses, and even saying "Merry Christmas" can be hazardous to your health.

To a secularist the brilliant answer to increasing gun violence in society is to ban guns from law-abiding people who don't commit gun violence (should we ban cell phones because texting while driving causes death?). Yet movies and musical artists romanticize the violent behavior. Hollywood stars tote and shoot guns on the movie set one day and then call for gun control the next day. They have no consciousness that their "art" is a major contributor to the chaos.

Being ubiquitous this constant show of violence "normalizes" aggressive activity. The numbers of weekly deaths in our big cities from illegal gun possession is more than alarming and is increasing at amazing speed. Perhaps we should not ban guns from law abiding citizens but ban the sight and use of guns in movies, music, and art in order to mitigate this negative behavior.

When someone recommends a movie for me to see the first question I ask is, "Are there any guns in it?" Of course I already know the answer is yes. It seems Hollywood can't make a movie today without guns, car chases, explosions, gratuitous sex, lots of cursing, and subtle acceptance of deviant behavior. This is the animal side of human behavior oozing its way out into the culture. Since I already know what's in the movie why should I watch it?

Needless to say, I haven't seen a Hollywood movie in over 30 years. Can't there be drama, can't there be an interesting story told, without the use of guns or bloodshed? Even before my current Jewish studies changed my perspective I knew this form of entertainment was harmful to the psyche.

I own a gun and I know others who do. None of us ever brandish the gun or handle it irresponsibly and I know of no one who has been shot by a gun. I carry the gun because the American culture has surrounded me with people who are constantly exercising their animal nature, glorifying and romanticizing it, so the chances of violent behavior being used against me is increasing every day. Almost all gun owners carry their weapon and also pray that they will never have to use it.

In reality the secular Jew, the JINO, has trapped himself.

You are a slave to the constant barrage of secular deviancy and potential danger surrounding you. The good news is that you are your own Pharaoh and there is an escape hatch. You just have to wriggle through it and you can. You don't have to convince Pharaoh with devastating miracles to let you go. You just have to convince yourself to let you go. If everyone could wriggle away from secularism, oh what a wonderful world this would be!

All you have to do is turn away from your current lifestyle for a short period of time each day to do something Jewish. And what you will see will be remarkable. A view of HASHEM is quite remarkable. So, on one hand you have a mundane life and on the other hand you can have amazing perceptions. With that in mind this new shift in your life should actually be quite stimulating and motivating. You already have the natural desire and "spark" within to move from the animal to the spiritual. Currently you just don't see it that way but your vision can change.

So, walk right into the desert with no food or water. HASHEM will be there with you.

CHAPTER XIV

Comparing Secular And Biblical perspectives

How do you know if something is right or wrong? Where do you get your values and morals?

The secular answer is, "I feel it in my heart. I trust my heart." Isn't that a beautiful notion? Spoken like an adorable child of 5 years old. And this adorable child of 5 years old, or 25 years old, or 45 years old has a heart than tells them that if you borrow something you return it right away. Or if you break something that belongs to someone else, you have it repaired.

But what if you neighbor's heart tells him Might is Right? He lives his concept of morals and values just like you live yours. When he borrows your lawnmower and refuses to return it or pay for the repair if it breaks down, he feels perfectly justified because he will punch you in the nose if you accuse him of not returning what's yours.

Who's to say your values (return things you borrow) are

higher, better, or more uplifting than his? Each one knows in their heart that they are "right." But which value lifts the individual at the same time lifting humanity? Which value lifts the individual without lifting anyone else? Who is the judge of values? It's likely from both perspectives that you and your neighbor won't be relating too much in the future and one of you may even move away in order to get away from such contrasting beliefs.

This is what yields from the Secular perspective, a mishmash of "if it feels good do it" values stemming from the Heart. But, few Hearts are the same.

There are two perspectives existent in the world: the Secular perspective and the Biblical perspective. If you don't live by one you live by the other. There is no sharing and it's impossible to have neither. In the examples above both are living two separate lifestyles guided from the same location, the Heart. But secular values have no "higher" constant. They are always in flux, changing, and "change" is not always good and can often be really bad. A decision made at 15 years old (my heart feels this way) will be different at 25 years old (now my heart feels that way) and different again at 45 years old (now my heart feels another way) all stemming from the same "heart" criteria.

At some point a higher *constant* becomes really attractive as it brings relief from ongoing change. The Biblical perspective is that higher constant. It's what tells you that borrowing without returning, or not repairing when you break something, is wrong. It has been wrong for thousands of years and will continue to be wrong for thousands of years. Right is right no matter what age you are.

The more you become "observant" or just simply "study" Judaism the more you begin to see the world within the Biblical perspective, relying on your understanding of the Ten Commandments. This happens automatically with almost no effort because things become so clear. You see secular people struggling with problems that just a little bit of religion in their lives would easily resolve.

Depending on how a secular person's heart feels that day, they make their decisions. Depending on what Jewish Sages have argued over for thousands of years, sifted down and expressed in the Torah, religiously Jewish people make their decisions. One is anchored on shifting sands, the other on bedrock.

For example, I know this secular man well into his seventies who is all alone because he spends all day thinking about how all of his family members always do things to make him unhappy. His family won't to talk to him anymore because he always gets mad at them for some past or current affront. It's a shame. If he were involved in Torah study he would know that instead of thinking about all the things that others have done to make *him* unhappy, he should think about all the things he could do to make *others* happy. This shift in perspective from Secular to Biblical would change his life immeasurably.

Suggesting to secular people to pray never works because you have to love HASHEM with all your heart and all your soul in order to be good at prayer. The secular haven't come to the realization of a higher source yet so although you know that prayer might help even a little it absolutely doesn't suit them. And the answer to their problem may not even be solved by prayer but by looking for solutions within a Biblical perspective of morals and values and consulting what the Torah has to say about the situation.

An example of this Biblical perspective is when a problem presents itself and you refer to the Ten Commandments in order to take action. At that point you make your decision based on your best interpretation of the Ten Commandments. Sometimes it works out great. But it's very possible that you might make the wrong decision. So if you do make a wrong decision just go ahead and admit it, learn from it, and hope that HASHEM will give merit for the effort. It's nice to think a forgiving HASHEM probably will.

The secular decision-making lifestyle is much different. There are never any wrong decisions made from the Secular perspective. Most secular people are *never* wrong and will *never* admit that they are wrong even when they *are* objectively wrong. Excuses, rationalizations, and avoidance of facts dominate their lives. If it's in their "Heart" then they are, by definition, in the Right. Period! And also, some might even think it's advantageous to find support in their decisions by consulting with Life Counselors, trendy pop advisors, Crystals (essentially rocks!), or other such oracle to substantiate what is in their Heart!

From the Biblical perspective being wrong is simply a part of life. Getting it right is a process of understanding. There is no shame in being wrong, only growth, and growth is not a bad thing. Consulting the Torah helps to get things right. On occasion the right thing to do might be dictated by only a sliver of interpretation. But on most occasions the Torah is quite clear. I've found religious people often admit their mistakes. It makes them reasonable and tolerant of other views and opinions.

I know several secular people who have never been wrong about anything in their entire lives. They know everything about everything. They have never and will never admit to being wrong even when they know they are. Being right is who they are. It gives them substance and stature in their own minds. But ultimately it's repulsive and, by the way, nobody likes to be around them.

The Heart can sometimes be an awful arbiter. The Heart makes "the ends justify the means" absolutely right all the time. "This is a good thing so I'll do a bad thing in order to bring about the good thing." This is common sense twisted. This Secular perspective told Stalin, Marx, Mao, Pol Pot, Hitler, and Castro that they were right in committing mass exterminations of humanity in order to bring about a more civil society. It's a wonderful headspace for one particular person to own but it's not real healthy for the rest of humanity around them.

The Biblical perspective explains how the ends do not justify the means. For instance, any means achieved through the murder of people is forbidden. Simply stated, life is sacred and must never be taken, the only exception being killing in your own self-defense. This is a wonderful headspace for each particular person to own and healthy for the rest of humanity.

Cheating in any form such as cheating on a test or cheating in an election is another example of the ends justifying the means. Whatever the ends, it is still an act of lying and stealing. Lying and stealing are the foundations of coveting and adultery. So cheating actually breaks four of the Ten Commandments!

The Secular perspective allows a sibling to steal an inheritance from a brother and sister. The sibling would never hold up a Brinks truck with an AK-47. But steal a half million dollars from siblings? No problem. They lie, steal, and cheat and their reasoning is full of "facts" and rationalizations but it's still theft nonetheless. That's why elder abuse is so prevalent. The excuses are ubiquitous and the prosecutions and convictions are rare in our current American culture.

The Secular perspective allows a nephew to renege on a monthly payback on a loan from his uncle. He simply stops paying. That nephew would never rip a Rolex watch from a passerby. But not live up to his obligations to a family member? No problem. And it's not *really* stealing because his "good intention" is to pay everything in full "next month." That's a perfect example of a secular rationalization because the repayment "next month" never happens. It's a lie in the moment that only proves itself a lie at some point in the future. But in the present it is not a lie because he "fully intends" to make good on the loan. And so, at the moment, there is no theft. It's a pretty clever system but also obviously disingenuous.

It would be totally unacceptable to Americans if their politicians took them to war only to grab the booty of the conquered nation. But steal from their fellow Americans with graft and corruption? No problem. I'm not sure where or when this form of theft, stealing from your own family/citizens, became "acceptable" with all the offered good intentions, unproven facts, excuses, and rationalizations but it's not a good thing. What I am sure of is that it is born from the Secular perspective that immediate gratification supersedes all else.

The Ten Commandments don't say, "Good Intentions Absolves Theft." And that's why really lousy federal legislation, spending money with little results, continues on without being cancelled. Cancelling it would admit poor results and that someone was wrong somewhere regardless of the good intentions. And, remember, secularists are *never* wrong.

Perhaps the incredible political split in the United States today is due to a battle between these two polar perspectives.

The Biblical perspective on the Commandment to "Honor Your Mother and Father" is a very direct example of a higher constant dictating to humanity. It doesn't say (as the Secular perspective through the Heart demands today), "give all your resources to your offspring so that their lives are better than yours were." Your Heart tells you that. I know people who spend $60,000 per year on college tuition for their children but refuse to contribute $6,000 per year towards the rent deficit that their parents have to scrape together.

The Torah doesn't say that you have to love your parents. You just have to "honor" them. That means making their lives as they age comfortable, less stressful in, at the very least, a physical way. Children should provide for their parents the resources for food, clothing, and/or shelter. They did it for you for at least two decades, now you do it for them for at least two decades. Plan for it. Budget for it. The Commandment is there for a reason, for your parents benefit and for your ultimate benefit, because one day you might need the financial help from your children. Meet the basic needs of your parents first, and then take care of your adult children.

One interesting story that Jews learn in their study is that before they became the "Chosen Ones" HASHEM offered the Torah to all the other peoples on planet Earth. The first group asked to see the Torah and read in the Ten Commandments "Do Not Steal." But they liked to steal so they turned the Torah down. The next group also asked to see what was in the Torah and read, "Do Not Commit Adultery." But they liked being adulterous so they turned the Torah down. And so it went with all the peoples of the Earth who found fault with some or all of the Commandments after reading them.

Lastly, HASHEM offered the Torah to the Jews. The Hebrews said, "we accept," without even reading what was in it. And so they committed themselves to the Torah's Ten Commandments sight unseen just because they knew that if a higher source were offering it, whatever it was, it was probably a good thing. That's how we became the "chosen people," almost (as we also could have said no) by default. So here we are.

And what a people we are! Israel is the home to the Jewish people. With all its "faults" it's still a nation that leads others by its Biblical perspective. Israel has a vibrant economy, it wins an inordinate amount of Nobel Prizes in Science, its agricultural advances are shared with other nations, and they are always among the first to send doctors and much-needed supplies to disaster areas around the world, even to places that their enemies occupy. These are just a few of the ways that Israel shows the world how the Biblical perspective brings HASHEM down into physical space. As a Jew I'm proud of that and so should you be proud.

So if you do nothing else as a Jew at least do your best to live by the Ten Commandments. Know what they are and study the depth of these ten rules for living. It's best for you and best for humanity around you. Your Heart can easily fool you and the Torah (yes, it's in there) actually admonishes Man from relying on the Heart.

The Biblical perspective is one of the main benefits of becoming more religiously Jewish. In Judaism, being religious does not necessarily mean praying 3 times per day, eating Kosher, or even observing the Holidays. Leave that for those who are so inclined. Study is also considered being religious. So, study! Then you'll be "spiritual *and* religious" and a better person for it.

CHAPTER XV

THE HISTORY OF PLANET EARTH

The joke is: they came to kill us, we won, we ate. The reality of history on Earth is: about every one hundred years Jewish people get massacred and then we start anew. Don't ask me why or how. It just is. It's disgusting.

It's my guess that that's what the Diaspora in America and around the world, is all about. It's an exile or physical dispersion so that Jews are not quite so concentrated in one place, like Israel, so that they can easily be annihilated. The next monster to have the great idea of ridding the planet of the Chosen People will have to recognize that there are just too many Jews located in too many places all around the world so the "final solution" would, ultimately, be impossible to complete. They should think of some other disgusting plan to occupy their time.

The "Old" Testament makes it pretty clear that if you don't follow the Ten Commandments, you are punished. As a culture when the Jews become idolatrous, they get smashed like the idols they worship are eventually smashed. Idolatry does not necessarily mean worshipping physical objects like crystals or statues. It also means worshipping the idols of fame, fortune, beauty, power, etc. The Ten Commandments #1: You shall have no other Gods before me.

Maybe that's why we are the Chosen People. We are the ones chosen to uphold a higher standard, issued by HASHEM, rather than other peoples of the Earth. And we have done that. Wouldn't you prefer to join this team? Or would you rather hang with the lower standard? Your obstinate refusal, or lack of energy towards Jewish ritual, to rise to the Divine, is the evil within you that you will eventually overcome. It's very important that you recognize who the Jewish people are, their destiny in the world, and your part in it. Your part in it is simply to join in.

The history of the Earth is pretty awful. It starts with cruelty and continues into all forms of deviant behavior. It got so bad at one point that HASHEM had to kill every living thing with a flood except for Noah and the other inhabitants of his Ark. HASHEM promised never to do that again but things naturally progressed on Earth back into cruelty and deviant behavior to the point where He selectively destroyed the cities of Sodom and Gomorrah and other nearby communities for the same reasons, descent into evil behavior too ghastly to allow.

Even in the Garden of Eden bad things happened. A snake seduced Eve. Cain killed his brother Abel. After leaving the Garden Jacob stole his brother's birthright. Joseph's brothers sold him into slavery. So if you have children in your home who aren't getting along, that's nothing new. What you learn in the Torah is that things have a way of working out, one way or the other, depending on the depth of your religious conviction. What's the depth of your religious conviction?

You'd think humanity would learn the lesson of believing vs. non-believing, but apparently not. Today cruelty and deviant behavior seem to exist almost everywhere we look. Death and destruction are ubiquitous. Do standards exist anywhere on the planet? Oh, yes they do, within the Torah when you walk through the doors of the synagogue.

Standards equal morals and values. The secular world has "standards" that are quite elusive. To name just a couple, "If it doesn't hurt anybody else you can do it" and "If the ends are good whatever the means are acceptable." According to whom? Usually, it's according to corrupt secular legislators who issue laws safeguarding these "values." And corrupt secular judges adjudicate disputes. Where's the divine in all this? When the United States of America was founded the Ten Commandments were posted in every courthouse. Now they are being removed. Is this a good thing or a bad thing? Are we to be reminded of high standards or are high standards to be covered up?

The height of secular standards and the solution to all problems in our culture today is to make so much money that you are immune to everything and everybody. Hasn't it been that way all through time? It's just that now it's easier to make that kind of big money and more people are doing it. How you make the big money is never an issue. Just make it.

At that point you have the power to avoid prosecution for any illegal behavior whatsoever and then you are free and have the capacity to make charity donations to display what a generous and wonderful person you are. The ends justify the means. Being immune to all laws and giving large charity donations are the ends, making the money through the importation of illegal drugs, political payoffs, insider information, and monopolies are the means.

There are people who have the wealth to own huge gated mansions and possess entire islands just so that they can sexually abuse underage females and avoid prosecution. Some people destroy subpoenaed evidence and walk away free as a bird. An election poll worker states proudly, "If the rules don't work, we don't follow them." There is no godliness, no high standard, in any of these people.

Elsewhere in the world Africa is a hot mess of low standards, raping minor children is just part of the cultural norm. Isn't it instructive that Christians, the non-secular, are being slaughtered and no one seems to care? China owns millions of Uyghur slaves. I can go on and on, but you get the picture. Earth is not a very nice place. It is kind of embarrassing actually that we humans haven't been able to do better.

So if you look at the whole ball of wax, the Jews seem to be the people who uphold higher standards more than most other people that currently exist on the planet today. They may not be upholding them high enough and they might be able to do a better job, but nevertheless they are at the pinnacle of the moral scale. Maybe that's why others try to destroy us every one hundred years. Jews are the "conscience" of the world. By reaching for the divine our standards are way higher than anything the secular world can imagine and legislate.

So now that you are aware of these things you have to make your choice. Do you want to be an average person in the middle of a heinous world, or would you rather be part of a higher calling? Just hanging between the two positions makes you part of the problem, not the solution.

Bad people like their cruelty and deviant behavior and have found ways to do it without paying a price. Additionally, they don't want to be told to stop the activities, that their behavior is wrong, and that the Torah forbids it, or that it's a "sin." They don't like to be told that they are being "judged" by some "higher power" they can't see or hear. They don't like it when there are people walking around the planet who look at their cruelty and deviant behavior and disapprove just by being who they are, living Torah, being Jewish.

Once you understand this, the discipline of living the Ten Commandments becomes the good and responsible thing to do in order to lift the moral score of life on Earth. But also it's a bit dangerous to be Jewish. Jews don't do the right thing for nothing or for some future reward. They do the right thing to do the right thing and in doing so they make the planet a better place to live in.

You should be proud of your simple Jewish mission to join other people who are doing the same thing, doing rituals of righteousness, reaching for the Divine, at all levels of reverence. This moves your own personal place higher on the spectrum of Jewish observance. No more Idiot Jew for you. It's a good thing. It's the right thing to do. Even if there is no such thing as a Judgment Day (and, significantly, Jewish sages say very little about that day), in your dying breath you will know that you contributed to raising the moral standing of a really bad place.

So join other Jews *this coming Friday* at sundown and just light the Shabbos candles already!

CHAPTER XVI

Judaism: Is It Really Such A Very, Very Deep Dive?

Yes, it is. But so what? Just dive as deep as is comfortable for you. You have the spirit within you as you so easily profess the feeling and you do. You know for certain that the feeling is real. HASHEM is ready and happy for whatever level of observance you decide to engage in. What fruit has your cold indifference to Judaism brought you? You can change that to warm enthusiasm for the Divine.

Throughout history there have been many Jews who do nothing but study, all day, from when they wake up in the morning to when they go to sleep at night. Historically, they were paid by their family and/or their community to do this in order to examine Jewish writings down to the finest points. And this has been going on for 2500 years. It's still going on in Israel today. That's how deep a dive Judaism is.

You don't have to do that, far from it. You can choose to study just one hour per day if that feels right for you. Don't feel like the ultra-Orthodox are "more" Jewish or you "less" Jewish. You are both Jewish, even those who do absolutely nothing everyday year after year are also Jewish. They, just like you, just haven't found their way yet. Some people don't really feel Jewish unless they make Aliyah, move to Israel. That's right for them. You can feel just as Jewish anywhere in America if moving to Israel is not for you. Become more Jewish than you are now is the point. Improving you and your everyday life is the point.

HASHEM doesn't measure your observance level so much as your effort level, and also your capacity to do good things in the world. Making the effort to add a touch of Jewish ritual into your life increases that capacity.

The Tanach, the 24 books of the Old Testament of the Jews, is over 1300 pages long in the English version. I decided I should read all of it. "What exactly is in this book," I wanted to know. You might not have the time or the patience to do that. I read about 6-10 pages per day, allotting an hour and usually finishing in 45 minutes, and I finished it in half a year. For me it was time well spent. At least now I can say I read it all (even though there was much I didn't understand).

For you maybe it's not worth your investment of time. But at least you can read the Torah, the first 5 books of the 24 of the Old Testament. It is "only" 370 pages, at 6-10 pages per day, finishing it takes less than 2 months. It's OK to miss a day here or there. I did. No big deal. You think HASHEM will hold it against you? It's a merit simply just to read the

Torah. Now I've done it several times and have studied it in "beginner" classes. It's a discovery blast! And remember, this athlete is no great student.

Since my Jewbie stage I've taken to reading the "Torah portion," parshah, each week. So, over the last seven years of my newfound "religious" life I've read the 300 pages of the Torah several times. Yes, the story gets a little old, but the lessons are always fresh and new each time I read through it.

According to Jewish tradition the five books of The Torah were written by HASHEM. The authors of the other nineteen books were human beings. In addition to this there have been 2500 years of "Commentaries." These were "clarifications" or "opinions" as to the meaning of chapters, lines, and even down to a particular word in the Torah written by "Sages," men of great intelligence and wisdom in their time. There are volumes and volumes of Commentaries.

So like I said, Judaism is a very, very, deep, deep dive. There is nothing on Earth that equals this level of study and examination. It's something you begin to recognize and take pride in being Jewish the more you appreciate its depth and longevity. There have always been great scholars such as in Rome and Greece and even in our modern day. But nothing comes close to the collaboration of great minds throughout millennia contained within Judaism.

Many people use the excuse that it's just *too* big. And it is. But that's no excuse for you to not glean *any* of it. You're not going to become a Rabbi. Really, it's no big deal to attend a

Friday night Shabbat Service for an hour. You'll meet some people, connect to HASHEM at whatever level, and feel good about yourself. One hour per week will make you much more Jewish than you are now, meaning that you will come to understand what righteousness really means. If you miss a Friday night here or there because something else more "exciting" is going on, don't worry about it. Go, do your other exciting thing. I can tell you, because it happened to me, that I began looking forward to Shabbat services rather than doing the other something else. There's a certain calmness achieved that is seductive.

When I first started going to Friday night services I would leave and go right to an expensive restaurant for a fine meal and knock back a couple of drinks. It was loud and interesting as it was a place where other single people would also eat. At one point early on I realized that I was feeling very relaxed and calm after services. Then I would take myself into a pit of assorted noises, activity, expectations, and disappointments. The alcohol took me further away from the good vibe the Shabbat service had deposited into me.

So, despite the excellent food and the excitement of the surroundings I asked myself, "What are you doing, Idiot. You're getting juiced at the service and then getting un-juiced at the restaurant." So I stopped going to the restaurant on Friday nights in order to maintain the special feeling of Shabbos. That's how things change in a small but profound way.

If all you do right now is light Chanukah candles once

per year, try going to a High Holy Service. If going to High Holy services is a little too "heavy" for you, buy a book. The biography of the Rebbe is a good place to begin. A Crash Course In Jewish History is another good starting point or any kind of Jewish history book that might interest you.

If you don't even light Chanukah candles then buy a Menorah and light Chanukah candles once per year. Doing this you'll be shocked to learn that the Jewish "day" begins on the "night" before. What's up with that? If you light the candle on the first "day" of Chanukah instead of the night before you'll be one candle late every day! Even so, just move yourself forward a little bit at a time. Meantime, you are becoming more Jewish.

If you begin to attend Friday night services, even once per month, charity opportunities will present themselves. This does not mean writing a check. It means delivering hot meals to the home bound, packing bags of food for the (Jewish and non-Jewish) needy, and doing other kinds of grunt work that helps the congregation provide for others. It's actually quite fun.

Your circle of friends will change. You won't be tossing everybody you know out the window. You'll be adding new people into your life, not necessarily rejecting the people you already have as friends.

Single men and women could even meet a Jewish partner, where they might ordinarily not, as they live in the secular pit. The more Jewish a woman is the more she reflects modesty and purity as opposed to overtly sexy and alluring. As men become more Jewish they realize that the former is much more attractive and long lasting than the latter. And the more Jewish a man is the more he reflects honesty and devotion as opposed to ego and domination. For both genders, who the person actually is becomes more important than their physical appearance.

It doesn't matter how old you are. Get started. You spend time in the gym, in the hair salon, in the clothing store, all to be healthy and to be the best you can be. Judaism never falls away through time. Whatever you learn today stays with you forever, makes you better. Don't wait until you are 63 years old like I did. And if you are older than that don't think it's too late. HASHEM is there, waiting, for any increase in observance at any age. HASHEM doesn't "need" you. You need HASHEM.

I began with the Ten Commandments. So as I moved through life and fashioned my actions in accordance with them I "sinned" much less. Sin in Judaism means that there is probably a better, higher, action you could have taken. It can be teeny tiny and it can be large. It can be acting in a gruff fashion with a checkout person instead of a smile and a good word or it could mean outright theft. Ultimately, HASHEM is the judge.

Whatever observance changes you make in your life now will help you now and later in life as your character advances. And don't do it for some unknown "hereafter" reasons. Do it for here and now. If there is a benefit in some kind of hereafter, then that's a bonus for then. However, it would be nice to know that as you become a better person your past transgressions might be forgiven by a higher source.

After reading 1300 pages of the Old Testament I came upon this, "Hezekiah prayed for them, saying, 'May the benevolent HASHEM grant atonement for whoever sets his heart to seek out God, HASHEM, the God of his forefathers...'"

CHAPTER XVII

THE TEN SUGGESTIONS: YOUR NEW JEWISH STRENGTHENING PROGRAM

I know that you are motivated to start being more of a Jew because you are reading this book. I've answered why you feel this way. I've told you the benefits of growing more into Judaism. We've explored who you are now, your place in the world, and who you can be. It's very important that you proceed from here in your own way. But I would be remiss in not giving you an outline of simple ways you can jumpstart the effort. So, here goes!

Whenever you enter any exercise program to get physically fit there is a certain kind of "start-up" costs that you have to invest. At the gym you have to buy a membership, hire a trainer to create a program, learn how to set the machines properly to your physique, be taught the correct mechanics of each exercise, buy the shoes, clothing, protein, and hydration necessities. You can figure a good $600-$800. Want to start bike riding? The bike will cost $800-$1200 and then there's the shoes, clothing, protein, and hydration necessities. Tennis? The rackets, lessons, shoes, clothing, protein, and hydration necessities will run you over $700. Golf? $500 just for the clubs. Well, you get the idea.

Your baby step exercise program into Judaism, getting spiritually fit, involves the same kind of start-up investment but the outlay will probably run you less than $400 over the course of the first year considering all the books and Jewish paraphernalia (candles, candles, lots of candles) you'll need to get started. It's a pretty good deal considering other disciplines you might choose to take up. But as you start purchasing things the whole "vibe" in your house will change. Jewish books on your reading table, Mezuzahs on the doors, candlesticks and candles, they all create a different feeling in your home. That feeling is you growing. Don't be self-conscious about it. It will calm you down and help you to make better decisions in your life. You are still the same person, just better.

So, the following are my Ten Suggestions, your new baby steps exercise program with comments/advice, that will get you quickly and safely on your way in your return to Judaism. It's not expensive and it's not all that difficult. GOOD LUCK!

1. Buy two candlesticks and Shabbat candles and light them every Friday night.
    a. You can buy them really cheap at Walmart or Amazon but I buy them at a Judaica store (a shop that sells Jewish things) or a kosher market. It "keeps the

The Ten Suggestions: Your New Jewish Strengthening Program

money in the family," the quality is there, and the vibe contained on the products is good.
   b. Learn the Shabbat prayer in both Hebrew and English. It's not long. Just do an Internet search for "Shabbat Prayer." The Hebrew is always given phonetically.
   c. Time: 1 minute, 4-5 minutes/monthly.

2. Buy two Mezuzahs and install them on your front door and your back door.
   a. Make sure the Mezuzahs that you buy contain "the scroll." Unfortunately, the scroll Mezuzahs are remarkably expensive. These can also be purchased at a Judaica store or a kosher market.
   b. You're supposed to kiss them with your fingers every time you walk in and out but it's no big deal if you don't.
   c. You are supposed to have one on every door inside your house, but again don't worry about it as the front and back doors are good enough.
   d. Time: To purchase and hang, 1 hour/once/forever.

3. Buy a book on Judaism and create a routine where you read 45-60 minutes daily, the same amount of time you would spend with your gym workouts.
   a. I started with "A Crash Course On Judaism," "Jew vs. Jew," and "The Rebbe" but you can start with anything.

b. I like to do my routine in the morning with coffee before I start my day as my brainpower is refreshed from sleep. You might prefer it at night before you go to sleep. It makes for sweet dreams. Try to make it a daily habit but if you miss a day or two don't get mad at yourself. Sometimes a break is good.

c. Time: 5-7 hours per week.

4. Go to a Friday night Shabbat service once per month or at least some kind of class on Judaism.

    a. Increase to weekly when you feel ready. Don't push it.
    b. Try several different synagogues starting with Reform and then going to Conservative. It's unlikely that you will hit just the right one for you on the first try. Keep trying.
    c. After services, if someone invites you to a Shabbat dinner say "Yes." And yes, you will feel uncomfortable throughout the whole thing because you know everybody knows you know nothing but it's food, wine, about 75-90 minutes long, very relaxed, and I can guarantee you that it's much less painful than a circumcision. So, do it.
    d. If there is a Chabad near you, check out their classes. This is what they specialize in as opposed to Synagogues that are involved in many, many other efforts.
    e. Time: 2-8 hours/month to attend Shabbat services including travel time there and back depending on whether you go once per month or weekly.

5. Begin making your Saturdays a "Special" day with family and/or friends.
   a. Make the day "different" from all other days of the week. If possible do absolutely no business whatsoever as it will still all be there on subsequent days thereafter. Stop yourself from even thinking about business. It's not easy to do, but very rewarding.
   b. Drive as little as possible and handle money as little as possible.
   c. Read, eat, and nap a lot. Our veterinarian limits our dog to one chew bone per week for digestive reasons so now it's become her weekly Shabbat bone!
   d. Start with observing just a Shabbat morning, then increase by adding a Shabbat afternoon to the Shabbat morning, then increase to ending both with a nice dinner with family and friends finishing one hour after sundown: a whole Shabbat day of 25 hours!
   e. It might take a year to get the whole thing going. So what? However long it takes within your comfort zone, that's how long it will take! HASHEM is in no rush and neither should you.

6. Memorize the Ten Commandments in the proper order (naturally there is significance in the order).
   a. Make sure to memorize the Jewish Ten Commandments as the Christian Ten Commandments differ in some words and order.

b. Study the depth of them either with a book recommended by a Rabbi or going to a class or both.
c. Everyone's memorization skills are different but I learned them in five days, 10 minutes per day, so I think it can easily be done in less than an hour total. I'm certain some people will have them down permanently in 15 minutes during one sitting.

7. Learn the Shema, the most important of all Jewish Prayers.
a. It's not long. Learn both the English and the Hebrew.
b. It can be found on the Internet.
c. You are supposed to say it in both Hebrew first and then English right when you wake up in the morning and right before you go to sleep at night. Just say it anytime once per day. That's good enough for now.
d. Time: 1 minute, 2 minutes/day, 14 minutes/week.

8. Buy a Siddur, the Jewish book of prayers for all occasions.
a. Available online but all Judaica stores have them.
b. Get a Rabbi to recommend a version he likes. My Orthodox Rabbi recommended the one by Jonathan Sacks so that's the one I own.
c. Get one that is written in both English and Hebrew.
d. I'm always surprised by how many times I actually open it, especially when I travel.
e. Time: Variable.

9. Buy two Votive candles and light them on each date that your parents passed on. If your parents are still alive, do it for your grandparents that have passed on. It's good for you to observe their memory and your children will witness you doing it and absorb it as a beneficial Jewish ritual.

   a. Votive candles burn for 24 hours and cost less than a can of tennis balls that lasts for only 2 hours and less than a sleeve of golf balls which, in my case, lasts about 16 holes/4 hours.
   b. Since these candles last for 24 hours don't forget to light them at sunset on the day before the anniversary of the death as the Jewish "day" begins at night on the day before.
   c. You can recite the prayer in either English or Hebrew or both because you now own a Siddur and the prayer honoring deceased loved ones is in there.
   d. Time: 1 minute/year/parent or grandparent.

10. Buy a Menorah for Chanukah and some candles.

    a. Spend some money on a nice Menorah. You'll own it forever.
    b. I'm replacing my Menorah with one that burns oil, preferred by the Orthodox, but you don't have to.
    c. Don't wait until the first day (remember, the night before is the first day) of Chanukah to buy candles.

The stores are likely out of them by then and when they are out it becomes a whole "panic" to find some.
- d. Don't buy cheap candles, as they don't burn well. A whole box of candles for the eight days of the holiday will run $5 for the cheap ones and $12 for better ones. Splurge!
- e. If the wicks on the candles aren't the same length go ahead and cut them to the same size. It will look better as they burn.
- f. You can say the short prayer in English or Hebrew or both while the candles are being lit because you now own a Siddur and it's in there. If you don't own a Siddur (yet!) the prayers can be found on the Internet.
- g. Leave the lighted Menorah near a window visible to people who might pass by and see it. It will lift them.
- h. The first candle is put all the way on the right end of the Menorah and all succeeding candles are added from there to the left.
- i. However, the leftmost candle, the newest one, is the one that should be lit first and light the others moving successively to the right.

Extra Credit #1: Attend High Holy Services.
- i. It's hard to find a ticket for these services because this is the one thing most JINOs do.
- ii. The tickets are usually very expensive.
- iii. It's the Day of Atonement when you are forgiven for

your sins so the services are long and some services go all day for two or three days.

iv. Everything stated i-iii are all true within all three Jewish denominations.

Extra Credit #2: Attend a Passover Seder.

i. Every Jew who has one is happy to have you join them.

ii. Invite yourself. They already would have invited you if they knew you had nowhere to go so it's OK.

Extra Credit #3: Make your own Seder.

i. Invite all the people you love (including me!).

You are now officially well on the way to being a real Jew, no longer a JINO or an Idiot Jew and you are now, every day, moving up the scale on the Jewish spectrum. Your life is now so much better and the world is now so much better. Welcome back and,

CONGRATULATIONS!!!

Postscript

Throughout the course of this book I've detailed many tidbits you probably didn't know about Judaism. Taken as a whole they are amazing tidbits. Study other cultures around the world at any time in history and you won't find one as grand as Jewish history. It's unnecessary to be conceited about it. It just is.

Additionally, you now know enough about Judaism to enter any Jewish Synagogue of any denomination knowing enough of the basics to not embarrass yourself. You can be confident of that. You might even know more than some people who have been observant for years! In the past your total ignorance really was a valid excuse not to pursue your birthright. *Now that excuse is no longer valid.*

Either you remain totally within the cold pit of secularism constantly shielding yourself from potential danger, or you begin to acknowledge your Creator with warm interest as He protects you on your way. The ball is now bouncing in your court.

To you a toast: L'chaim! (which means) To Life, Health, and Well-Being!

ADDENDUM

The Ten Commandments

The short version:

1) Believe in One God.

2) Do not serve idols.

3) Do not take the name of God in vain.

4) Remember the Sabbath day.

5) Honor thy father and mother.

6) Do not murder.

7) Do not commit adultery.

8) Do not steal.

9) Do not lie.

10) Do not covet.

The long version:

1. I am the Lord Your God, who brought you out of the land of Egypt, out of the house of bondage.

2. You shall have no other gods beside Me. You shall not make for yourself any graven image, nor any manner of likeness, of any thing that is heaven above, or that is in the earth

beneath, or that is in the water under the earth. You shall not bow down to them, nor serve them, for I, the Lord Your God, am a jealous God, visiting the iniquity of the fathers upon the children unto the third and fourth generation.

3. You shall not take the name of the Lord Your God in vain; for the Lord will not hold him guiltless that takes His name in vain.

4. Remember the Sabbath, to keep it holy. Six days you shall labor, and do all your work; but the seventh day is a Sabbath unto the Lord Your God, in it you shall not do any manner of work, you, nor your son, nor your daughter, nor your man-servant, nor your maid-servant, nor your cattle, nor your stranger that is within your gates; for in six days the Lord made heaven and earth, the sea, and all that is in them, and rested on the seventh day. Wherefore the Lord blessed the Sabbath day, and made it holy.

5. Honor your father and your mother, that your days may be long upon the land which the Lord God gives you.

6. You shall not murder.

7. You shall not commit adultery.

8. You shall not steal.

9. You shall not bear false witness against your neighbor.

10. You shall not covet your neighbor's house, nor his wife, his man-servant, his maid-servant, nor his ox, nor his ass, nor anything that is your neighbor's.